Unity 2018 Artificial Intelligence Cookbook

Second Edition

Over 90 recipes to build and customize AI entities for your games with Unity

Jorge Palacios

BIRMINGHAM - MUMBAI

Unity 2018 Artificial Intelligence Cookbook
Second Edition

Commissioning Editor: Kunal Chaudhari
Acquisition Editor: Akshay Ghadi
Content Development Editor: Flavian Vaz
Technical Editor: Sachin Sunilkumar
Copy Editor: Safis Editing
Project Coordinator: Devanshi Doshi
Proofreader: Safis Editing
Indexer: Priyanka Dhadke
Graphics: Jason Monteiro
Production Coordinator: Shraddha Falebhai

First published: March 2016
Second edition: August 2018

Production reference: 1240818

Published by Packt Publishing Ltd.
Livery Place
35 Livery Street
Birmingham
B3 2PB, UK.

ISBN 978-1-78862-617-0

www.packtpub.com

To my parents, Betty and Elieser.
They have given me all their support for several years,
and believed in me every step of the way.
Words cannot express how grateful I am for having them in my life.
This work is proof that dreams can be achieved when you turn them into goals.

Thanks to my partner in bits and codes, Christian Chomiak.
His support and feedback is always appreciated on every adventure,
and every algorithm. Let's co-author the next book!

"If I have seen further it is by standing on the shoulders of giants."
– Isaac Newton

I'll be forever grateful to Ricardo Monascal and Carlos Pérez.
Their support, friendship, and guidance allowed me to become
the developer that I am today. I have seen further because of you.

`mapt.io`

Mapt is an online digital library that gives you full access to over 5,000 books and videos, as well as industry leading tools to help you plan your personal development and advance your career. For more information, please visit our website.

Why subscribe?

- Spend less time learning and more time coding with practical eBooks and Videos from over 4,000 industry professionals

- Improve your learning with Skill Plans built especially for you

- Get a free eBook or video every month

- Mapt is fully searchable

- Copy and paste, print, and bookmark content

PacktPub.com

Did you know that Packt offers eBook versions of every book published, with PDF and ePub files available? You can upgrade to the eBook version at `www.PacktPub.com` and as a print book customer, you are entitled to a discount on the eBook copy. Get in touch with us at `service@packtpub.com` for more details.

At `www.PacktPub.com`, you can also read a collection of free technical articles, sign up for a range of free newsletters, and receive exclusive discounts and offers on Packt books and eBooks.

Contributors

About the author

Jorge Palacios is a software and game developer with a BS in computer science and eight years of professional experience. He's been developing games for the last five years in different roles, from tool developer to lead programmer. Mainly focused on artificial intelligence and gameplay programming, he is currently working with Unity and HTML5. He's also a game-programming instructor, speaker, and game-jam organizer.

About the reviewer

Dr. Davide Aversa holds a PhD in artificial intelligence and an MSc in artificial intelligence and robotics from the University of Rome, "La Sapienza," in Italy. He has a strong interest in artificial intelligence for the development of interactive virtual agents and Procedural Content Generation (PCG). He serves as a peer reviewer in video game-related conferences, such as the IEEE conference on Computational Intelligence and Games (CIG) and he also regularly participates in game-jam contests.

Packt is searching for authors like you

If you're interested in becoming an author for Packt, please visit `authors.packtpub.com` and apply today. We have worked with thousands of developers and tech professionals, just like you, to help them share their insight with the global tech community. You can make a general application, apply for a specific hot topic that we are recruiting an author for, or submit your own idea.

Table of Contents

Preface

When we think about **artificial intelligence** (**AI**), a lot of topics may come to mind, from simple behaviors such as following or escaping from the player, through the classic chess-rival AI, to state-of-the-art techniques in machine learning or procedural content generation.

Talking about Unity means talking about game development democratization. Thanks to its ease of use, fast-paced technological improvements, ever-growing community of developers, and new cloud services, Unity has become one of the most important pieces of game industry software.

With all that in mind, the main goal of writing this book is to offer you, the reader, both technical insight into Unity, following best practices and conventions, and theoretical knowledge that helps you grasp AI concepts and techniques, so you can get the best of both worlds for your own personal and professional development.

This cookbook will introduce you to the tools you need to build great AI, either for creating better enemies, polishing that final boss, or even building your own customized AI engine. It aims to be your one-stop reference for developing AI techniques in Unity.

Welcome to an exciting journey that combines a variety of things that means a lot to me as a professional and human being; programming, game development, AI, and sharing knowledge with other developers. I cannot stress how humbled and happy I am to be read by you right now, and grateful to the team at Packt for this formidable opportunity. I hope this material helps you not only take your Unity and AI skills to new levels, but also deliver that feature that will engage players with your game.

Who this book is for

This book is intended for those who already have a basic knowledge of Unity and are eager to get more tools under their belt to solve AI and gameplay-related problems.

What this book covers

Chapter 1, *Behaviors – Intelligent Movement*, explores some of the most interesting movement algorithms based on the steering behavior principles developed by Craig Reynolds and work from Ian Millington. They act as a foundation for most of the AI used in advanced games and other algorithms that rely on movement, such as the family of path-finding algorithms.

Chapter 2, *Navigation*, covers path-finding algorithms for navigating complex scenarios. It will include some ways of representing the world using different kinds of graph structure, and several algorithms for finding a path, each aimed to different situations.

Chapter 3, *Decision Making*, explains different decision-making techniques that are flexible enough to adapt to different types of games, and robust enough to let us build modular decision-making systems.

Chapter 4, *The New NavMesh API*, shows the inner workings of the NavMesh API introduced in Unity 5.6, and explains how it enables us to grasp the power of the NavMesh engine and tune it in real time.

Chapter 5, *Coordination and Tactics*, deals with a number of different recipes for coordinating different agents as a whole organism, such as formations and techniques that allow us make tactical decisions based on graphs, such as waypoints and influence maps.

Chapter 6, *Agent Awareness*, explores different ways to simulate sense stimuli on an agent. We will learn how to use tools we already know to create these simulations: colliders and graphs.

Chapter 7, *Board Games and Applied Search AI*, covers a family of algorithms for developing board games, as well as turn-based-game techniques for creating AI.

Chapter 8, *Learning Techniques*, explores the field of machine learning. It will give us a great head-start in our endeavor to learn and apply machine learning techniques into our games.

Chapter 9, *Procedural Content Generation*, explores different techniques for enabling replayability in our games by creating content procedurally. It will give us some pointers in the right direction for different types of content.

Chapter 10, *Miscellaneous*, introduces new techniques and uses algorithms that we will have learned in previous chapters to create new behaviors that don't quite fit in a definite category.

To get the most out of this book

Anyone with a strong programming background will be able to get the most out of this book. However, readers that also have strong foundations in comp-sci will benefit greatly from the set of implementations in Unity.

Before you start, it is important to know about programming, data structures, and the basic foundations of C#. We assume that you feel comfortable creating scripts components in Unity, and have developed some prototypes in the past.

We believe that you will get the most out of this book if you already have an idea of the modules for beginner and intermediate gameplay scripting available at `https://unity3d.com/learn/tutorials/s/scripting`.

We have developed this book using Unity, Visual Studio Community, and Visual Studio Code. The latter shows better performance and behaves in the same way in Windows and Mac operating systems. The first would be our choice for a Windows-only development environment.

Download the example code files

You can download the example code files for this book from your account at `www.packtpub.com`. If you purchased this book elsewhere, you can visit `www.packtpub.com/support` and register to have the files emailed directly to you.

You can download the code files by following these steps:

1. Log in or register at `www.packtpub.com`.
2. Select the **SUPPORT** tab.
3. Click on **Code Downloads & Errata**.
4. Enter the name of the book in the **Search** box and follow the onscreen instructions.

Once the file is downloaded, please make sure that you unzip or extract the folder using the latest version of:

- WinRAR/7-Zip for Windows
- Zipeg/iZip/UnRarX for Mac
- 7-Zip/PeaZip for Linux

The code bundle for the book is also hosted on GitHub at `https://github.com/PacktPublishing/Unity-2018-Artificial-Intelligence-Cookbook-Second-Edition`. In case there's an update to the code, it will be updated on the existing GitHub repository.

We also have other code bundles from our rich catalog of books and videos available at `https://github.com/PacktPublishing/`. Check them out!

Download the color images

We also provide a PDF file that has color images of the screenshots/diagrams used in this book. You can download it here: `https://www.packtpub.com/sites/default/files/downloads/Unity2018ArtificialIntelligenceCookbookSecondEdition_ColorImages.pdf`.

Conventions used

There are a number of text conventions used throughout this book.

`CodeInText`: Indicates code words in text, database table names, folder names, filenames, file extensions, pathnames, dummy URLs, user input, and Twitter handles. Here is an example: "`Agent` is the main component, and it makes use of behaviors in order to create intelligent movement."

A block of code is set as follows:

```
public override void Awake()
{
    base.Awake();
    targetAgent = target.GetComponent<Agent>();
    targetAux = target;
    target = new GameObject();
}
```

When we wish to draw your attention to a particular part of a code block, the relevant lines or items are set in bold:

```
public override void Awake()
{
    base.Awake();
    targetAgent = target.GetComponent<Agent>();
    targetAux = target;
    target = new GameObject();
}
```

Bold: Indicates a new term, an important word, or words that you see onscreen. For example, words in menus or dialog boxes appear in the text like this. Here is an example: "We also need to have the **Agent** script component attached to them"

 Warnings or important notes appear like this.

 Tips and tricks appear like this.

Sections

In this book, you will find several headings that appear frequently (*Getting ready, How to do it..., How it works..., There's more...,* and *See also*).

To give clear instructions on how to complete a recipe, use these sections as follows:

Getting ready

This section tells you what to expect in the recipe and describes how to set up any software or any preliminary settings required for the recipe.

How to do it...

This section contains the steps required to follow the recipe.

How it works...

This section usually consists of a detailed explanation of what happened in the previous section.

There's more...

This section consists of additional information about the recipe in order to make you more knowledgeable about the recipe.

See also

This section provides helpful links to other useful information for the recipe.

Get in touch

Feedback from our readers is always welcome.

General feedback: Email `feedback@packtpub.com` and mention the book title in the subject of your message. If you have questions about any aspect of this book, please email us at `questions@packtpub.com`.

Errata: Although we have taken every care to ensure the accuracy of our content, mistakes do happen. If you have found a mistake in this book, we would be grateful if you would report this to us. Please visit `www.packtpub.com/submit-errata`, selecting your book, clicking on the Errata Submission Form link, and entering the details.

Piracy: If you come across any illegal copies of our works in any form on the internet, we would be grateful if you would provide us with the location address or website name. Please contact us at `copyright@packtpub.com` with a link to the material.

If you are interested in becoming an author: If there is a topic that you have expertise in and you are interested in either writing or contributing to a book, please visit `authors.packtpub.com`.

Reviews

Please leave a review. Once you have read and used this book, why not leave a review on the site that you purchased it from? Potential readers can then see and use your unbiased opinion to make purchase decisions, we at Packt can understand what you think about our products, and our authors can see your feedback on their book. Thank you!

For more information about Packt, please visit `packtpub.com`.

Behaviors - Intelligent Movement 1

In this chapter, we will develop AI algorithms for movement by covering the following recipes:

- Creating the behaviors template
- Pursuing and evading
- Adjusting the agent for physics
- Arriving and leaving
- Facing objects
- Wandering around
- Following a path
- Avoiding agents
- Avoiding walls
- Blending behaviors by weight
- Blending behaviors by priority
- Shooting a projectile
- Predicting a projectile's landing spot
- Targeting a projectile
- Creating a jump system

Introduction

Unity has been one of the most popular game engines for quite a while now, and it's probably the *de facto* game development tool for indie developers, not only because of its business model, which has a low entry barrier, but also because of its robust project editor, year-by-year technological improvements, and, most importantly, its ease of use and an ever-growing community of developers around the globe.

Thanks to Unity's heavy lifting behind the scenes (rendering, physics, integration, and cross-platform deployment, to name but a few) it's possible for us to focus on creating the AI systems that will bring our games to life, creating great real-time experiences in the blink of an eye.

The goal of this book is to give you the tools to build great AI, create better enemies, polish that final boss, or even build your own customized AI engine.

In this chapter, we will start by exploring some of the most interesting movement algorithms based on the steering behavior principles developed by Craig Reynolds, along with work from Ian Millington. These recipes are the stepping stones for most of the AI used in advanced games and other algorithms that rely on movement, such as the family of path-finding algorithms.

Creating the behaviors template

Before creating our behaviors, we need to code the stepping stones that help us to create not only intelligent movement, but also help us to build a modular system to change and add these behaviors. We will create custom data types and base classes for most of the algorithms covered in this chapter.

Getting ready

Our first step is to remember the update functions' order of execution:

- `Update`
- `LateUpdate`

How to do it...

We need to create three classes, Steering, AgentBehaviour, and Agent:

1. Steering serves as a custom data type for storing the movement and rotation of the agent:

    ```
    using UnityEngine;
    public class Steering
    {
      public float angular;
      public Vector3 linear;
      public Steering ()
      {
        angular = 0.0f;
        linear = new Vector3();
      }
    }
    ```

2. AgentBehaviour is the template class for most of the behaviors covered in this chapter:

    ```
    using UnityEngine;
    public class AgentBehaviour : MonoBehaviour
    {
      public GameObject target;
      protected Agent agent;
      public virtual void Awake ()
      {
        agent = gameObject.GetComponent<Agent>();
      }
      public virtual void Update ()
      {
          agent.SetSteering(GetSteering());
      }
      public virtual Steering GetSteering ()
      {
        return new Steering();
      }
    }
    ```

3. Finally, Agent is the main component, and it makes use of behaviors in order to create intelligent movement. Create the file and its bare bones:

    ```
    using UnityEngine;
    using System.Collections;
    public class Agent : MonoBehaviour
    ```

```
    {
        public float maxSpeed;
        public float maxAccel;
        public float orientation;
        public float rotation;
        public Vector3 velocity;
        protected Steering steering;
        void Start ()
        {
            velocity = Vector3.zero;
            steering = new Steering();
        }
        public void SetSteering (Steering steering)
        {
            this.steering = steering;
        }
    }
```

4. Next, we code the `Update` function, which handles the movement according to the current value:

```
public virtual void Update ()
{
    Vector3 displacement = velocity * Time.deltaTime;
    orientation += rotation * Time.deltaTime;
    // we need to limit the orientation values
    // to be in the range (0 - 360)
    if (orientation < 0.0f)
        orientation += 360.0f;
    else if (orientation > 360.0f)
        orientation -= 360.0f;
    transform.Translate(displacement, Space.World);
    transform.rotation = new Quaternion();
    transform.Rotate(Vector3.up, orientation);
}
```

5. Finally, we implement the `LateUpdate` function, which takes care of updating the steering for the next frame according to the current frame's calculations:

```
public virtual void LateUpdate ()
{
    velocity += steering.linear * Time.deltaTime;
    rotation += steering.angular * Time.deltaTime;
    if (velocity.magnitude > maxSpeed)
    {
        velocity.Normalize();
        velocity = velocity * maxSpeed;
    }
```

```
if (steering.angular == 0.0f)
{
    rotation = 0.0f;
}
if (steering.linear.sqrMagnitude == 0.0f)
{
    velocity = Vector3.zero;
}
steering = new Steering();
}
```

How it works...

The idea is to be able to delegate the movement's logic inside the `GetSteering()` function on the behaviors that we will later build, simplifying our agent's class to a main calculation based on those.

Besides, we are guaranteed to be able to set the agent's steering value before it is used thanks to Unity script and function execution orders.

There's more...

This is a component-based approach, which means that we must remember to always have an `Agent` script attached to `GameObject` for the behaviors to work as expected.

See also

For further information on Unity's game loop and the execution order of functions and scripts, please refer to the official documentation available online at these links:

- http://docs.unity3d.com/Manual/ExecutionOrder.html
- https://docs.unity3d.com/Manual/class-MonoManager.html

Pursuing and evading

Pursuing and evading are great behaviors to start with because they rely on the most basic behaviors and extend their functionality by predicting the target's next step.

Getting ready

We need a couple of basic behaviors called `Seek` and `Flee`; place them right after the `Agent` class in the scripts' execution order.

The following is the code for the `Seek` behavior:

```
using UnityEngine;
using System.Collections;
public class Seek : AgentBehaviour
{
    public override Steering GetSteering()
    {
        Steering steering = new Steering();
        steering.linear = target.transform.position - transform.position;
        steering.linear.Normalize();
        steering.linear = steering.linear * agent.maxAccel;
        return steering;
    }
}
```

Also, we need to implement the `Flee` behavior:

```
using UnityEngine;
using System.Collections;
public class Flee : AgentBehaviour
{
    public override Steering GetSteering()
    {
        Steering steering = new Steering();
        steering.linear = transform.position - target.transform.position;
        steering.linear.Normalize();
        steering.linear = steering.linear * agent.maxAccel;
        return steering;
    }
}
```

How to do it...

Pursue and Evade are essentially the same algorithm, but differ in terms of the base class they derive from:

1. Create the Pursue class, derived from Seek, and add the attributes for the prediction:

```
using UnityEngine;
using System.Collections;

public class Pursue : Seek
{
    public float maxPrediction;
    private GameObject targetAux;
    private Agent targetAgent;
}
```

2. Implement the Awake function in order to set up everything according to the real target:

```
public override void Awake() { base.Awake(); targetAgent =
target.GetComponent<Agent>(); targetAux = target; target = new
GameObject(); }
```

3. Implement the OnDestroy function for properly handling the internal object:

```
void OnDestroy ()
{
    Destroy(targetAux);
}
```

4. Implement the GetSteering function:

```
public override Steering GetSteering()
{
    Vector3 direction = targetAux.transform.position -
transform.position;
    float distance = direction.magnitude;
    float speed = agent.velocity.magnitude;
    float prediction;
    if (speed <= distance / maxPrediction)
        prediction = maxPrediction;
    else
        prediction = distance / speed;
    target.transform.position = targetAux.transform.position;
    target.transform.position += targetAgent.velocity * prediction;
```

```
            return base.GetSteering();
    }
```

5. To create the `Evade` behavior, the procedure is just the same, but it takes into account the fact that `Flee` is the parent class:

```
public class Evade : Flee
{
    // everything stays the same
}
```

How it works...

These behaviors rely on `Seek` and `Flee` and take into consideration the target's velocity in order to predict where it will go next, and they aim at that position using an internal extra object.

Adjusting the agent for physics

We learned how to implement simple behaviors for our agents. However, we also need to take into consideration that our games will probably need the help of the physics engine in Unity. In that case, we need to take into consideration whether our agents have the `RigidBody` component attached to them, and adjust our implementation accordingly.

Getting ready

Our first step is to remember the execution order of event functions, but now we also consider `FixedUpdate`, because we're handling behaviors on top of the physics engine:

- `FixedUpdate`
- `Update`
- `LateUpdate`

How to do it...

This recipe entails adding changes to our `Agent` class.

1. Go to the `Agent` class.

2. Add a member variable for storing the rigid body component's reference:

```
private Rigidbody aRigidBody;
```

3. Get the reference to the rigid body component in the `Start` function:

```
aRigidBody = GetComponent<Rigidbody>();
```

4. Implement a function for transforming an orientation value to a vector:

```
public Vector3 OriToVec(float orientation)
{
  Vector3 vector = Vector3.zero;
  vector.x = Mathf.Sin(orientation * Mathf.Deg2Rad) * 1.0f;
  vector.z = Mathf.Cos(orientation * Mathf.Deg2Rad) * 1.0f;
  return vector.normalized;
}
```

5. Add the following two lines at the beginning of the `Update` function:

```
public virtual void Update ()
{
  if (aRigidBody == null)
    return;
  // ... previous code
```

6. Define the `FixedUpdate` function:

```
public virtual void FixedUpdate()
{
  if (aRigidBody == null)
    return;
  // next step
}
```

7. Continue implementing the `FixedUpdate` function:

```
Vector3 displacement = velocity * Time.deltaTime;
orientation += rotation * Time.deltaTime;
if (orientation < 0.0f)
  orientation += 360.0f;
else if (orientation > 360.0f)
  orientation -= 360.0f;
// The ForceMode will depend on what you want to achieve
// We are using VelocityChange for illustration purposes
aRigidBody.AddForce(displacement, ForceMode.VelocityChange);
Vector3 orientationVector = OriToVec(orientation);
aRigidBody.rotation = Quaternion.LookRotation(orientationVector,
```

```
Vector3.up);
```

How it works...

We added a member variable for storing the reference to a possible rigid body component, and also implemented `FixedUpdate`, similar to `Update`, but taking into consideration that we need to apply force to the rigid body instead of translating the object ourselves, because we're working on top of Unity's physics engine.

Finally, we created a simple validation at the beginning of each function so they're called only when it applies.

See also

For further information on the execution order of event functions, please refer to official Unity documentation:

- `https://docs.unity3d.com/Manual/ExecutionOrder.html`

Arriving and leaving

Similar to `Seek` and `Flee`, the idea behind these algorithms is to apply the same principles and extend the functionality to a point where the agent stops automatically after a condition is met, either being close to its destination (arrive), or far enough from a dangerous point (leave).

Getting ready

We need to create one file for the `Arrive` and `Leave` algorithms respectively, and remember to set their custom execution order.

How to do it...

They use the same approach, but in terms of implementation, the name of the member variables change, as well as some computations in the first half of the `GetSteering` function:

1. First, implement the `Arrive` behavior with its member variables to define the radius for stopping (target) and slowing down:

```
using UnityEngine;
using System.Collections;

public class Arrive : AgentBehaviour
{
    public float targetRadius;
    public float slowRadius;
    public float timeToTarget = 0.1f;
}
```

2. Create the `GetSteering` function:

```
public override Steering GetSteering()
{
    // code in next steps
}
```

3. Define the first half of the `GetSteering` function, in which we compute the desired speed depending on the distance from the target according to the radii variables:

```
Steering steering = new Steering();
Vector3 direction = target.transform.position - transform.position;
float distance = direction.magnitude;
float targetSpeed;
if (distance < targetRadius)
    return steering;
if (distance > slowRadius)
    targetSpeed = agent.maxSpeed;
else
    targetSpeed = agent.maxSpeed * distance / slowRadius;
```

4. Define the second half of the `GetSteering` function, in which we set the steering value and clamp it according to the maximum speed:

```
Vector3 desiredVelocity = direction;
desiredVelocity.Normalize();
desiredVelocity *= targetSpeed;
steering.linear = desiredVelocity - agent.velocity;
steering.linear /= timeToTarget;
if (steering.linear.magnitude > agent.maxAccel)
{
    steering.linear.Normalize();
    steering.linear *= agent.maxAccel;
```

```
    }
    return steering;
```

5. To implement `Leave`, change the name of the member variables:

```
using UnityEngine;
using System.Collections;

public class Leave : AgentBehaviour
{
    public float escapeRadius;
    public float dangerRadius;
    public float timeToTarget = 0.1f;
}
```

6. Define the first half of the `GetSteering` function:

```
Steering steering = new Steering();
Vector3 direction = transform.position - target.transform.position;
float distance = direction.magnitude;
if (distance > dangerRadius)
    return steering;
float reduce;
if (distance < escapeRadius)
    reduce = 0f;
else
    reduce = distance / dangerRadius * agent.maxSpeed;
float targetSpeed = agent.maxSpeed - reduce;
```

7. And finally, the second half of `GetSteering` stays just the same.

How it works...

After calculating the direction to go in, the next calculations are based on two radii distances in order to know when to go full throttle, slow down, and stop; that's why we have several `if` statements. In the `Arrive` behavior, when the agent is too far, we aim for full throttle, progressively slow down when inside the proper radius, and finally stop when close enough to the target. The inverse method applies to `Leave`:

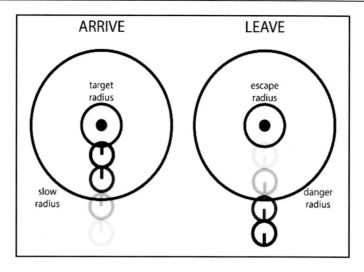

A visual reference for the Arrive and Leave behaviors

Facing objects

Real-world aiming, just like in combat simulators, works a little differently to the widely-used *automatic* aiming process in almost every game. Imagine that you need to implement an agent controlling a tank turret or a humanized sniper; that's when this recipe comes in handy.

Getting ready

We need to make some modifications to our `AgentBehaviour` class:

1. Add new member values to limit some of the existing ones:

```
public float maxSpeed;
public float maxAccel;
public float maxRotation;
public float maxAngularAccel;
```

2. Add a function called `MapToRange`. This function helps in finding the actual direction of rotation after two orientation values are subtracted:

```
public float MapToRange (float rotation) {
    rotation %= 360.0f;
    if (Mathf.Abs(rotation) > 180.0f) {
        if (rotation < 0.0f)
            rotation += 360.0f;
        else
            rotation -= 360.0f;
    }
    return rotation;
}
```

3. Also, we need to create a basic behavior called `Align` that is the stepping stone for the facing algorithm. It uses the same principle as `Arrive`, but only in terms of rotation:

```
using UnityEngine;
using System.Collections;

public class Align : AgentBehaviour
{
    public float targetRadius;
    public float slowRadius;
    public float timeToTarget = 0.1f;

    public override Steering GetSteering()
    {
        Steering steering = new Steering();
        float targetOrientation =
target.GetComponent<Agent>().orientation;
        float rotation = targetOrientation - agent.orientation;
        rotation = MapToRange(rotation);
        float rotationSize = Mathf.Abs(rotation);
        if (rotationSize < targetRadius)
            return steering;
        float targetRotation;
        if (rotationSize > slowRadius)
            targetRotation = agent.maxRotation;
        else
            targetRotation = agent.maxRotation * rotationSize /
slowRadius;
        targetRotation *= rotation / rotationSize;
        steering.angular = targetRotation - agent.rotation;
        steering.angular /= timeToTarget;
        float angularAccel = Mathf.Abs(steering.angular);
```

```
        if (angularAccel > agent.maxAngularAccel)
        {
            steering.angular /= angularAccel;
            steering.angular *= agent.maxAngularAccel;
        }
        return steering;
    }
}
```

How to do it...

We can now proceed to implement our facing algorithm that derives from `Align`:

1. Create the `Face` class along with a private auxiliary target member variable:

```
using UnityEngine;
using System.Collections;

public class Face : Align
{
    protected GameObject targetAux;
}
```

2. Override the `Awake` function to set up everything and swap references:

```
public override void Awake()
{
    base.Awake();
    targetAux = target;
    target = new GameObject();
    target.AddComponent<Agent>();
}
```

3. Also, implement the `OnDestroy` function to handle references and avoid memory issues:

```
void OnDestroy ()
{
    Destroy(target);
}
```

4. Finally, define the `GetSteering` function:

```
public override Steering GetSteering()
{
    Vector3 direction = targetAux.transform.position -
transform.position;
    if (direction.magnitude > 0.0f)
    {
        float targetOrientation = Mathf.Atan2(direction.x,
direction.z);
        targetOrientation *= Mathf.Rad2Deg;
        target.GetComponent<Agent>().orientation =
targetOrientation;
    }
    return base.GetSteering();
}
```

How it works...

The algorithm computes the internal target orientation according to the vector between the agent and the real target. Then, it just delegates the work to its parent class.

Wandering around

This technique works like a charm for random crowd simulations, animals, and almost any kind of NPC that requires random movement when idle.

Getting ready

We need to add another function to our `AgentBehaviour` class called `OriToVec`, which converts an orientation value to a vector:

```
public Vector3 GetOriAsVec (float orientation) {
    Vector3 vector  = Vector3.zero;
    vector.x = Mathf.Sin(orientation * Mathf.Deg2Rad) * 1.0f;
    vector.z = Mathf.Cos(orientation * Mathf.Deg2Rad) * 1.0f;
    return vector.normalized;
}
```

How to do it...

We can regard it as a big three-step process in which we first manipulate the internal target position in a parameterized random way, face that position, and move accordingly:

1. Create the `Wander` class deriving from `Face`:

```
using UnityEngine;
using System.Collections;

public class Wander : Face
{
    public float offset;
    public float radius;
    public float rate;
}
```

2. Define the `Awake` function in order to set up the internal target:

```
public override void Awake()
{
    target = new GameObject();
    target.transform.position = transform.position;
    base.Awake();
}
```

3. Define the `GetSteering` function:

```
public override Steering GetSteering()
{
    Steering steering = new Steering();
    float wanderOrientation = Random.Range(-1.0f, 1.0f) * rate;
    float targetOrientation = wanderOrientation +
agent.orientation;
    Vector3 orientationVec = OriToVec(agent.orientation);
    Vector3 targetPosition = (offset * orientationVec) +
transform.position;
    targetPosition = targetPosition + (OriToVec(targetOrientation)
* radius);
    targetAux.transform.position = targetPosition;
    steering = base.GetSteering();
    steering.linear = targetAux.transform.position -
transform.position;
    steering.linear.Normalize();
    steering.linear *= agent.maxAccel;
    return steering;
}
```

How it works...

The behavior takes two radii in order into consideration to get a random position to go next, looks toward that random point, and converts the computed orientation into a direction vector in order to advance:

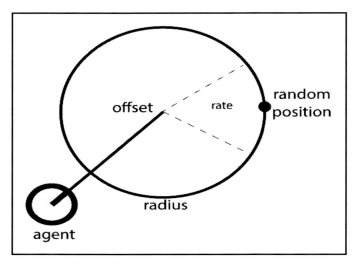

A visual description of the parameters for creating the Wander behavior

Following a path

There are times when we need scripted routes, and it's simply inconceivable to do it entirely by code. Imagine you're working on a stealth game. Would you code a route for every single guard? This technique will help you build a flexible path system for those situations.

Getting ready

We need to define a custom data type called `PathSegment`:

```
using UnityEngine;
using System.Collections;

public class PathSegment
{
```

```
public Vector3 a;
public Vector3 b;

public PathSegment () : this (Vector3.zero, Vector3.zero){}
public PathSegment (Vector3 a, Vector3 b)
{
    this.a = a;
    this.b = b;
}
}
```

How to do it...

This is a long recipe that could be regarded as a big two-step process. First, we build the Path class, which abstracts points in the path from their specific spatial representations, and then we build the PathFollower behavior that makes use of that abstraction in order to get actual spatial points to follow:

1. Create the Path class, which consists of nodes and segments; only the nodes are public and are assigned manually:

```
using UnityEngine;
using System.Collections;
using System.Collections.Generic;

public class Path : MonoBehaviour
{
    public List<GameObject> nodes;
    List<PathSegment> segments;
}
```

2. Define the Start function to set the segments when the scene starts:

```
void Start()
{
    segments = GetSegments();
}
```

3. Define the GetSegments function to build the segments from the nodes:

```
public List<PathSegment> GetSegments ()
{
    List<PathSegment> segments = new List<PathSegment>();
    int i;
    for (i = 0; i < nodes.Count - 1; i++)
    {
```

```
        Vector3 src = nodes[i].transform.position;
        Vector3 dst = nodes[i+1].transform.position;
        PathSegment segment = new PathSegment(src, dst);
        segments.Add(segment);
    }
    return segments;
}
```

4. Define the first function for abstraction, which is called `GetParam`:

```
public float GetParam(Vector3 position, float lastParam)
{
    // body
}
```

5. We need to find out the segment the agent is closest to:

```
float param = 0f;
PathSegment currentSegment = null;
float tempParam = 0f;
foreach (PathSegment ps in segments)
{
    tempParam += Vector3.Distance(ps.a, ps.b);
    if (lastParam <= tempParam)
    {
        currentSegment = ps;
        break;
    }
}
if (currentSegment == null)
    return 0f;
```

6. Given the current position, we need to work out the direction to go to:

```
Vector3 currPos = position - currentSegment.a;
Vector3 segmentDirection = currentSegment.b - currentSegment.a;
segmentDirection.Normalize();
```

7. Find the point in the segment using vector projection:

```
Vector3 pointInSegment = Vector3.Project(currPos,
segmentDirection);
```

8. Finally, `GetParam` returns the next position to reach along the path:

```
param = tempParam - Vector3.Distance(currentSegment.a,
currentSegment.b);
```

```
param += pointInSegment.magnitude;
return param;
```

9. Define the `GetPosition` function:

```
public Vector3 GetPosition(float param)
{
    // body
}
```

10. Given the current location along the path, we find the corresponding segment:

```
Vector3 position = Vector3.zero;
PathSegment currentSegment = null;
float tempParam = 0f;
foreach (PathSegment ps in segments)
{
    tempParam += Vector3.Distance(ps.a, ps.b);
    if (param <= tempParam)
    {
        currentSegment = ps;
        break;
    }
}
if (currentSegment == null)
    return Vector3.zero;
```

11. `GetPosition` converts the parameter as a spatial point and returns it:

```
Vector3 segmentDirection = currentSegment.b - currentSegment.a;
segmentDirection.Normalize();
tempParam -= Vector3.Distance(currentSegment.a, currentSegment.b);
tempParam = param - tempParam;
position = currentSegment.a + segmentDirection * tempParam;
return position;
```

12. Create the `PathFollower` behavior, which derives from `Seek` (remember to set the order of execution):

```
using UnityEngine;
using System.Collections;

public class PathFollower : Seek
{
    public Path path;
    public float pathOffset = 0.0f;
    float currentParam;
}
```

13. Implement the `Awake` function to set the target:

```
public override void Awake()
{
    base.Awake();
    target = new GameObject();
    currentParam = 0f;
}
```

14. The final step is to define the `GetSteering` function that relies on the abstraction created by the `Path` class to set the target position and apply `Seek`:

```
public override Steering GetSteering()
{
    currentParam = path.GetParam(transform.position, currentParam);
    float targetParam = currentParam + pathOffset;
    target.transform.position = path.GetPosition(targetParam);
    return base.GetSteering();
}
```

How it works...

We use the `Path` class in order to have a movement guideline. It is the cornerstone, because it relies on `GetParam` to map an offset point to follow in its internal guideline, and it also uses `GetPosition` to convert that referential point to a position in the three-dimensional space along the segments.

The path-following algorithm just makes use of the path's functions in order to get a new position, update the target, and apply the `Seek` behavior.

There's more...

It's important to take into account the order in which the nodes are linked in the inspector for the path to work as expected. A practical way to achieve this is to manually name the nodes with a reference number:

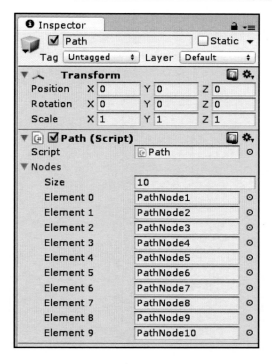

An example of a path set up in the Inspector window

Also, we could define the OnDrawGizmos function in order to have a better visual reference of the path:

```
void OnDrawGizmos ()
{
    Vector3 direction;
    Color tmp = Gizmos.color;
    Gizmos.color = Color.magenta;//example color
    int i;
    for (i = 0; i < nodes.Count - 1; i++)
    {
        Vector3 src = nodes[i].transform.position;
        Vector3 dst = nodes[i+1].transform.position;
        direction = dst - src;
        Gizmos.DrawRay(src, direction);
    }
    Gizmos.color = tmp;
}
```

Avoiding agents

In crowd-simulation games, it would be unnatural to see agents behaving entirely like particles in a physics-based system. The goal of this recipe is to create an agent capable of mimicking our peer-evasion movement.

Getting ready

We need to create a tag called **Agent** and assign it to those game objects that we would like to avoid, and we also need to have the **Agent** script component attached to them:

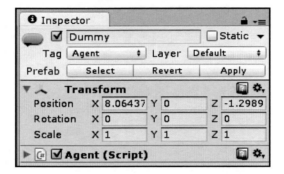

Example of how the Inspector window of a dummy agent should appear

Take a look on the following:

- Tag: Agent (created by us)
- Agent component is attached (the one created by us)

How to do it...

This recipe will entail creating a new agent behavior:

1. Create the `AvoidAgent` behavior, which is composed of a collision avoidance radius and the list of agents to avoid:

```
using UnityEngine;
using System.Collections;
using System.Collections.Generic;

public class AvoidAgent : AgentBehaviour
```

```
{
    public float collisionRadius = 0.4f;
    GameObject[] targets;
}
```

2. Implement the `Start` function in order to set the list of agents according to the tag we created earlier:

```
void Start ()
{
    targets = GameObject.FindGameObjectsWithTag("Agent");
}
```

3. Define the `GetSteering` function:

```
public override Steering GetSteering()
{
    // body
}
```

4. Add the following variables to the compute distances and velocities from agents that are nearby:

```
Steering steering = new Steering();
float shortestTime = Mathf.Infinity;
GameObject firstTarget = null;
float firstMinSeparation = 0.0f;
float firstDistance = 0.0f;
Vector3 firstRelativePos = Vector3.zero;
Vector3 firstRelativeVel = Vector3.zero;
```

5. Find the closest agent that is prone to collision with the current one:

```
foreach (GameObject t in targets)
{
    Vector3 relativePos;
    Agent targetAgent = t.GetComponent<Agent>();
    relativePos = t.transform.position - transform.position;
    Vector3 relativeVel = targetAgent.velocity - agent.velocity;
    float relativeSpeed = relativeVel.magnitude;
    float timeToCollision = Vector3.Dot(relativePos, relativeVel);
    timeToCollision /= relativeSpeed * relativeSpeed * -1;
    float distance = relativePos.magnitude;
    float minSeparation = distance - relativeSpeed *
timeToCollision;
    if (minSeparation > 2 * collisionRadius)
        continue;
    if (timeToCollision > 0.0f && timeToCollision < shortestTime)
```

```
        {
            shortestTime = timeToCollision;
            firstTarget = t;
            firstMinSeparation = minSeparation;
            firstRelativePos = relativePos;
            firstRelativeVel = relativeVel;
        }
    }
```

6. If there is one that is prone to collision, then move away:

```
if (firstTarget == null)
    return steering;
if (firstMinSeparation <= 0.0f || firstDistance < 2 *
collisionRadius)
    firstRelativePos = firstTarget.transform.position;
else
    firstRelativePos += firstRelativeVel * shortestTime;
firstRelativePos.Normalize();
steering.linear = -firstRelativePos * agent.maxAccel;
return steering;
```

How it works...

Given a list of agents, we take into consideration which one is closest, and, if it is close enough, we make it so that the agent tries to escape from the expected route of that first one according to its current velocity, so that they don't collide.

There's more...

This behavior works well when combined with other behaviors using blending techniques (some are included in this chapter); otherwise, it's a starting point for your own collision avoidance algorithms.

Avoiding walls

In this recipe, we will implement a behavior that imitates our own ability to evade walls. That is, seeing what we have in front of us that could be considered as a wall or obstacle, and walk around it using a safety margin, trying to maintain our principal direction at the same time.

Getting ready

This technique uses the `RaycastHit` structure and the `Raycast` function from the physics engine, so it's recommended that you look at the documents for a refresher in case you're a little rusty on the subject.

How to do it...

Thanks to our previous hard work, this recipe is a short one:

1. Create the `AvoidWall` behavior derived from `Seek`:

```
using UnityEngine;
using System.Collections;

public class AvoidWall : Seek
{
    // body
}
```

2. Include the member variables for defining the safety margin and the length of the ray to cast:

```
public float avoidDistance;
public float lookAhead;
```

3. Define the `Awake` function to set up the target:

```
public override void Awake()
{
    base.Awake();
    target = new GameObject();
}
```

4. Define the `GetSteering` function required for future steps:

```
public override Steering GetSteering()
{
    // body
}
```

5. Declare and set the variable needed for ray casting:

```
Steering steering = new Steering();
Vector3 position = transform.position;
Vector3 rayVector = agent.velocity.normalized * lookAhead;
Vector3 direction = rayVector;
RaycastHit hit;
```

6. Cast the ray and make the proper calculations if a wall is hit:

```
if (Physics.Raycast(position, direction, out hit, lookAhead))
{
    position = hit.point + hit.normal * avoidDistance;
    target.transform.position = position;
    steering = base.GetSteering();
}
return steering;
```

How it works...

We cast a ray in front of the agent, and when the ray collides with a wall, the target object is placed in a new position, with consideration given to its distance from the wall and the safety distance declared, delegating the steering calculations to the Seek behavior; this creates the illusion of the agent avoiding the wall.

There's more...

We could extend this behavior by adding more rays, such as whiskers, in order to achieve better accuracy. Also, it is usually paired with other movement behaviors, such as Pursue, using blending:

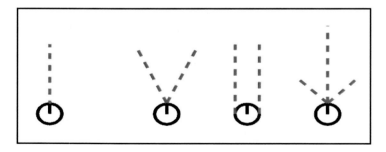

The original ray cast and possible extensions for more precise wall avoidance

See also

For further information on the `RaycastHit` structure and the `Raycast` function, please refer to the official documentation available online at these links:

- `http://docs.unity3d.com/ScriptReference/RaycastHit.html`
- `http://docs.unity3d.com/ScriptReference/Physics.Raycast.html`

Blending behaviors by weight

The blending techniques allow you to add behaviors and mix them without creating new scripts every time you need a new type of hybrid agent.

This is one of the most powerful techniques in this chapter, and it's probably the most widely-used behavior-blending approach because of its power and the low cost of implementation.

Getting ready

We must add a new member variable to our `AgentBehaviour` class called `weight` and preferably assign a default value. In this case, this is `1.0f`. We should refactor the `Update` function to incorporate `weight` as a parameter for the `Agent` class's `SetSteering` function. All in all, the new `AgentBehaviour` class should look something like this:

```
public class AgentBehaviour : MonoBehaviour
{
    public float weight = 1.0f;

    // ... the rest of the class

    public virtual void Update ()
    {
        agent.SetSteering(GetSteering(), weight);
    }
}
```

How to do it...

We just need to change the `SetSteering` function's signature and definition:

```
public void SetSteering (Steering steering, float weight)
{
    this.steering.linear += (weight * steering.linear);
    this.steering.angular += (weight * steering.angular);
}
```

How it works...

The weights are used to amplify the `steering` behavior result, and they're added to the main steering structure.

There's more...

The weights don't necessarily need to add up to `1.0f`. The `weight` parameter is a reference for defining the relevance that the `steering` behavior will have among other parameters.

See also

In this project, there is an example of avoiding walls, which is worked out using weighted blending.

Blending behaviors by priority

Sometimes, weighted blending is not enough because heavyweight behaviors dilute the contribution of the lightweights, but those behaviors need to do their part too. That's when priority-based blending comes into play, applying a cascading effect from high-priority to low-priority behaviors.

Getting ready

This approach is very similar to the one used in the previous recipe. We must add a new member variable to our `AgentBehaviour` class. We should also refactor the `Update` function to incorporate `priority` as a parameter to the `Agent` class's `SetSteering` function. The new `AgentBehaviour` class should look something like this:

```
public class AgentBehaviour : MonoBehaviour
{
    public int priority = 1;
    // ... everything else stays the same
    public virtual void Update ()
    {
        agent.SetSteering(GetSteering(), priority);
    }
}
```

How to do it...

Now, we need to make some changes to the `Agent` class:

1. Add a new namespace from the library:

   ```
   using System.Collections.Generic;
   ```

2. Add the member variable for the minimum steering value to consider a group of behaviors:

   ```
   public float priorityThreshold = 0.2f;
   ```

3. Add the member variable for holding the group of behavior results:

   ```
   private Dictionary<int, List<Steering>> groups;
   ```

4. Initialize the variable in the `Start` function:

   ```
   groups = new Dictionary<int, List<Steering>>();
   ```

5. Modify the `LateUpdate` function so that the steering variable is set by calling `GetPrioritySteering`:

   ```
   public virtual void LateUpdate ()
   {
       // funnelled steering through priorities
       steering = GetPrioritySteering();
   ```

```
        groups.Clear();
        // ... the rest of the computations stay the same
        steering = new Steering();
    }
```

6. Modify the `SetSteering` function's signature and definition to store the steering values in their corresponding priority groups:

```
public void SetSteering (Steering steering, int priority)
{
    if (!groups.ContainsKey(priority))
    {
        groups.Add(priority, new List<Steering>());
    }
    groups[priority].Add(steering);
}
```

7. Finally, implement the `GetPrioritySteering` function to funnel the steering group:

```
private Steering GetPrioritySteering ()
{
    Steering steering = new Steering();
    float sqrThreshold = priorityThreshold * priorityThreshold;
    foreach (List<Steering> group in groups.Values)
    {
        steering = new Steering();
        foreach (Steering singleSteering in group)
        {
            steering.linear += singleSteering.linear;
            steering.angular += singleSteering.angular;
        }
        if (steering.linear.sqrMagnitude > sqrThreshold ||
                Mathf.Abs(steering.angular) > priorityThreshold)
        {
            return steering;
        }
    }
    return steering;
}
```

How it works...

By creating priority groups, we blend behaviors that are common to one another, and the first group, in which the steering value exceeds the threshold, is selected. Otherwise, steering from the lowest-priority group is chosen.

There's more...

We could extend this approach by mixing it with weighted blending, so we would have a more robust architecture, achieving extra precision in the way the behaviors impact on the agent at every priority level:

```
foreach (Steering singleSteering in group)
{
    steering.linear += singleSteering.linear * weight;
    steering.angular += singleSteering.angular * weight;
}
```

See also

There is an example of avoiding walls using priority-based blending in this project.

Shooting a projectile

This is the stepping stone for scenarios where we want to have control over gravity-reliant objects, such as balls and grenades, so we can then predict the projectile's landing spot or be able to effectively shoot a projectile at a given target.

Getting ready

This recipe differs a little bit as it doesn't rely on the base `AgentBehaviour` class.

How to do it...

1. Create the `Projectile` class, along with its member variables, to handle the physics:

```
using UnityEngine;
using System.Collections;

public class Projectile : MonoBehaviour
{
    private bool set = false;
    private Vector3 firePos;
    private Vector3 direction;
    private float speed;
    private float timeElapsed;
}
```

2. Define the `Update` function:

```
void Update ()
{
    if (!set)
        return;
    timeElapsed += Time.deltaTime;
    transform.position = firePos + direction * speed * timeElapsed;
    transform.position += Physics.gravity * (timeElapsed *
timeElapsed) / 2.0f;
    // extra validation for cleaning the scene
    if (transform.position.y < -1.0f)
        Destroy(this.gameObject);// or set = false; and hide it
}
```

3. Finally, implement the `Set` function in order to fire the game object (for example, calling it after it is instantiated in the scene):

```
public void Set (Vector3 firePos, Vector3 direction, float speed)
{
    this.firePos = firePos;
    this.direction = direction.normalized;
    this.speed = speed;
    transform.position = firePos;
    set = true;
}
```

How it works...

This behavior uses high school physics in order to generate the parabolic movement.

There's more...

We could also take another approach: implementing public properties in the script or declaring member variables as public, and instead of calling the Set function, having the script disabled by default in the prefab and enabling it after all the properties have been set. That way, we could easily apply the object pool pattern.

See also

For further information on the object pool pattern, please refer to the following Wikipedia article and the official Unity technologies video tutorial available online:

- http://en.wikipedia.org/wiki/Object_pool_pattern
- http://unity3d.com/learn/tutorials/modules/beginner/live-training-arch ive/object-pooling

Predicting a projectile's landing spot

After a projectile is shot by the player, agents (our AI) need to either avoid it or look for it. For example, the agents need to run from a grenade to be kept alive, or run towards a soccer ball to take control. In either case, it's important for the agents to predict the projectile's landing spot to make decisions.

In this recipe, we will learn how to calculate such landing spots.

Getting ready

Before we get into predicting the landing position, it's important to know the time left before it hits the ground (or reaches a certain position). Thus, instead of creating new behaviors, we need to update the Projectile class.

How to do it...

1. First, we need to add the `GetLandingTime` function to compute the landing time:

```
public float GetLandingTime (float height = 0.0f)
{
    Vector3 position = transform.position;
    float time = 0.0f;
    float valueInt = (direction.y * direction.y) * (speed * speed);
    valueInt = valueInt - (Physics.gravity.y * 2 * (position.y -
height));
    valueInt = Mathf.Sqrt(valueInt);
    float valueAdd = (-direction.y) * speed;
    float valueSub = (-direction.y) * speed;
    valueAdd = (valueAdd + valueInt) / Physics.gravity.y;
    valueSub = (valueSub - valueInt) / Physics.gravity.y;
    if (float.IsNaN(valueAdd) && !float.IsNaN(valueSub))
        return valueSub;
    else if (!float.IsNaN(valueAdd) && float.IsNaN(valueSub))
        return valueAdd;
    else if (float.IsNaN(valueAdd) && float.IsNaN(valueSub))
        return -1.0f;
    time = Mathf.Max(valueAdd, valueSub);
    return time;
}
```

2. Now, we add the `GetLandingPos` function to predict the landing spot:

```
public Vector3 GetLandingPos (float height = 0.0f)
{
    Vector3 landingPos = Vector3.zero;
    float time = GetLandingTime();
    if (time < 0.0f)
        return landingPos;
    landingPos.y = height;
    landingPos.x = firePos.x + direction.x * speed * time;
    landingPos.z = firePos.z + direction.z * speed * time;
    return landingPos;
}
```

How it works...

First, we are solving the equation from the previous recipe for a fixed height, and, given the projectile's current position and speed, we are able to get the time at which the projectile will reach the given height.

There's more...

Remember to take into account the NaN validation. It's placed that way because there may be one, two, or no solutions to the equation. Furthermore, when the landing time is less than zero, it means the projectile won't be able to reach the target height.

Targeting a projectile

Just as it's important to predict a projectile's landing point, it's also important to develop intelligent agents capable of aiming projectiles. It wouldn't be fun if our rugby-player agents weren't capable of passing the ball.

Getting ready

Just as in the previous recipe, we only need to expand the Projectile class.

How to do it...

Thanks to our previous hard work, this recipe is a real piece of cake:

1. Create the GetFireDirection function:

```
public static Vector3 GetFireDirection (Vector3 startPos, Vector3
endPos, float speed)
{
    // body
}
```

2. Solve the corresponding quadratic equation:

```
Vector3 direction = Vector3.zero;
Vector3 delta = endPos - startPos;
float a = Vector3.Dot(Physics.gravity, Physics.gravity);
float b = -4 * (Vector3.Dot(Physics.gravity, delta) + speed *
speed);
float c = 4 * Vector3.Dot(delta, delta);
if (4 * a * c > b * b)
    return direction;
float time0 = Mathf.Sqrt((-b + Mathf.Sqrt(b * b - 4 * a * c)) /
(2*a));
float time1 = Mathf.Sqrt((-b - Mathf.Sqrt(b * b - 4 * a * c)) /
(2*a));
```

3. If shooting the projectile is feasible given the parameters, return a non-zero
   `direction` **vector**:

```
float time;
if (time0 < 0.0f)
{
    if (time1 < 0)
        return direction;
    time = time1;
}
else
{
    if (time1 < 0)
        time = time0;
    else
        time = Mathf.Min(time0, time1);
}
direction = 2 * delta - Physics.gravity * (time * time);
direction = direction / (2 * speed * time);
return direction;
```

How it works...

Given a fixed speed, we solve the corresponding quadratic equation in order to obtain the
desired direction (when at least a single one-time value is available), which doesn't need to
be normalized because we already normalized the vector while setting up the projectile.

There's more...

Take account of the fact that we are returning a *blank* direction when the time is negative; it means that the speed is not sufficient. One way to overcome this is to define a function that tests different speeds and then shoot the projectile.

Another relevant improvement is to add an extra parameter of the type `bool` for those cases when we have two valid times (which means two possible arcs), and we need to shoot over an obstacle such as a wall:

```
if (isWall)
    time = Mathf.Max(time0, time1);
else
    time = Mathf.Min(time0, time1);
```

Creating a jump system

Imagine that we're developing a cool action game where the player is capable of escaping using cliffs and rooftops. In that case, the enemies need to be able to chase the player and be smart enough to discern whether to take the jump and gauge how to do it.

Getting ready

We need to create a basic matching-velocity algorithm and the notion of jump pads and landing pads in order to emulate velocity math so that we can reach them.

The following is the code for the `VelocityMatch` behavior:

```
using UnityEngine;
using System.Collections;

public class VelocityMatch : AgentBehaviour {
    public float timeToTarget = 0.1f;

    public override Steering GetSteering()
    {
        Steering steering = new Steering();
        steering.linear = target.GetComponent<Agent>().velocity -
agent.velocity;
        steering.linear /= timeToTarget;
        if (steering.linear.magnitude > agent.maxAccel)
            steering.linear = steering.linear.normalized * agent.maxAccel;
```

```
            steering.angular = 0.0f;
            return steering;
        }
    }
```

Also, it's important to create a data type called `JumpPoint`:

```
using UnityEngine;
using System.Collections;

public class JumpPoint
{
    public Vector3 jumpLocation;
    public Vector3 landingLocation;

    //The change in position from jump to landing
    public Vector3 deltaPosition;

    public JumpPoint () : this (Vector3.zero, Vector3.zero)
    {
    }

    public JumpPoint(Vector3 a, Vector3 b)
    {
        this.jumpLocation = a;
        this.landingLocation = b;
        this.deltaPosition = this.landingLocation - this.jumpLocation;
    }
}
```

How to do it...

1. Create the `Jump` script along with its member variables:

```
using UnityEngine;
using System.Collections;

public class Jump : VelocityMatch
{
    public JumpPoint jumpPoint;
    public float maxYVelocity;
    public Vector3 gravity = new Vector3(0, -9.8f, 0);
    bool canAchieve = false;
}
```

2. Implement the `SetJumpPoint` function:

```
public void SetJumpPoint(Transform jumpPad, Transform landingPad)
{
    jumpPoint = new JumpPoint(jumpPad.position,
landingPad.position);
}
```

3. Add a function to calculate the target:

```
protected void CalculateTarget()
{
    target = new GameObject();
    target.AddComponent<Agent>();
    target.transform.position = jumpPoint.jumpLocation;
    //Calculate the first jump time
    float sqrtTerm = Mathf.Sqrt(2f * gravity.y *
jumpPoint.deltaPosition.y + maxYVelocity * agent.maxSpeed);
    float time = (maxYVelocity - sqrtTerm) / gravity.y;
    //Check if we can use it, otherwise try the other time
    if (!CheckJumpTime(time))
    {
        time = (maxYVelocity + sqrtTerm) / gravity.y;
    }
}
```

4. Implement the `CheckJumpTime` function, to decide whether it's worth taking the jump:

```
private bool CheckJumpTime(float time)
{
    //Calculate the planar speed
    float vx = jumpPoint.deltaPosition.x / time;
    float vz = jumpPoint.deltaPosition.z / time;
    float speedSq = vx * vx + vz * vz;
    //Check it to see if we have a valid solution
    if (speedSq < agent.maxSpeed * agent.maxSpeed)
    {
        target.GetComponent<Agent>().velocity = new Vector3(vx, 0f,
vz);
        canAchieve = true;
        return true;
    }
    return false;
}
```

5. Finally, define the `GetSteering` function:

```
public override Steering GetSteering()
{
    Steering steering = new Steering();
    if (target == null)
    {
        CalculateTarget();
    }
    if (!canAchieve)
    {
        return steering;
    }
    //Check if we've hit the jump point
    if (Mathf.Approximately((transform.position -
target.transform.position).magnitude, 0f) &&
        Mathf.Approximately((agent.velocity -
target.GetComponent<Agent>().velocity).magnitude, 0f))
    {
        // call a jump method based on the Projectile behaviour
        return steering;
    }
    return base.GetSteering();
}
```

How it works...

The algorithm takes into account the agent's velocity and calculates whether it can reach the landing pad or not. If it judges that the agent can, it tries to match the vertical velocity while seeking the landing pad's position.

2
Navigation

In this chapter, we will cover the following recipes:

- Representing the world with grids
- Representing the world with points of visibility
- Representing the world with a self-made navigation mesh
- Finding your way out of a maze with DFS
- Finding the shortest path in a grid with BFS
- Finding the shortest path with Dijkstra
- Finding the best-promising path with A*
- Improving A* for memory: IDA*
- Planning navigation in several frames: time-sliced search
- Smoothing a path

Introduction

In this chapter, we will learn path-finding algorithms for navigating complex scenarios. Game worlds are usually complex structures, be it a maze, an open world, and everything in between. That's why we need different techniques for approaching these kinds of problems.

We'll learn some ways of representing the world using different kinds of graph structures, and several algorithms for finding a path, each aimed at different situations.

It is worth mentioning that path-finding algorithms rely on techniques such as `Seek` and `Arrive`, learned in the previous chapter, in order to navigate the map.

Representing the world with grids

A grid is the most widely-used structure for representing worlds in games because it is easy to implement and visualize. However, we will lay the foundations for advanced graph representations while learning the basis of graph theory and its properties.

Getting ready

First, we need to create an abstract class, `Graph`, declaring the virtual methods that every graph representation implements. It is done this way because no matter how the vertices and edges are represented internally, the path-finding algorithms remain high level, thereby avoiding implementation of the algorithms for each type of graph representation.

This class works as a parent class for the different representations to be learned in the chapter and is a good starting point if you want to implement graph representations not covered in the book.

Then, we will implement a graph sub-class that handles itself internally as a grid.

How to do it...

The following code is for the `Graph` class:

1. Create the backbone with the member values:

```
using UnityEngine;
using System.Collections;
using System.Collections.Generic;

public abstract class Graph : MonoBehaviour
{
    public GameObject vertexPrefab;
    protected List<Vertex> vertices;
    protected List<List<Vertex>> neighbours;
    protected List<List<float>> costs;
    // next steps
}
```

2. Define the `Start` function:

```
public virtual void Start()
{
    Load();
}
```

3. Define the `Load` function, mentioned previously:

```
public virtual void Load() { }
```

4. Implement the function for getting the graph's size:

```
public virtual int GetSize()
{
    if (ReferenceEquals(vertices, null))
        return 0;
    return vertices.Count;
}
```

5. Define the function for finding the nearest vertex given a position:

```
public virtual Vertex GetNearestVertex(Vector3 position)
{
    return null;
}
```

6. Implement the function for getting the vertex given its ID:

```
public virtual Vertex GetVertexObj(int id)
{
    if (ReferenceEquals(vertices, null) || vertices.Count == 0)
        return null;
    if (id < 0 || id >= vertices.Count)
        return null;
    return vertices[id];
}
```

7. Implement the function for retrieving a vertex's neighbors:

```
public virtual Vertex[] GetNeighbours(Vertex v)
{
    if (ReferenceEquals(neighbours, null) || neighbours.Count == 0)
        return new Vertex[0];
    if (v.id < 0 || v.id >= neighbours.Count)
        return new Vertex[0];
    return neighbours[v.id].ToArray();
}
```

We also need a `Vertex` class; use the following code:

```
using UnityEngine;
using System.Collections.Generic;
[System.Serializable]
public class Vertex : MonoBehaviour
{
    public int id;
    public List<Edge> neighbours;
    [HideInInspector]
    public Vertex prev;
}
```

We need to create a class for storing a vertex's neighbors with the costs. This class will be called `Edge`. Let's implement it:

1. Create the `Edge` class, deriving from `IComparable`:

```
using System;

[System.Serializable]
public class Edge : IComparable<Edge>
{
    public float cost;
    public Vertex vertex;
    // next steps
}
```

2. Implement its constructor:

```
public Edge(Vertex vertex = null, float cost = 1f)
{
    this.vertex = vertex;
    this.cost = cost;
}
```

3. Implement the comparison member function:

```
public int CompareTo(Edge other)
{
    float result = cost - other.cost;
    int idA = vertex.GetInstanceID();
    int idB = other.vertex.GetInstanceID();
    if (idA == idB)
        return 0;
    return (int)result;
}
```

4. Implement the function for comparing two edges:

```
public bool Equals(Edge other)
{
    return (other.vertex.id == this.vertex.id);
}
```

5. Override the function for comparing two objects:

```
public override bool Equals(object obj)
{
    Edge other = (Edge)obj;
    return (other.vertex.id == this.vertex.id);
}
```

6. Override the function for retrieving the hash code. This is necessary when overriding the previous member function:

```
public override int GetHashCode()
{
    return this.vertex.GetHashCode();
}
```

Besides creating the previous classes, it's important to define a couple of prefabs based on the cube primitive in order to visualize the ground (maybe a low-height cube) and walls or obstacles. The prefab for the ground is assigned to the `vertexPrefab` variable and the wall prefab is assigned to the `obstaclePrefab` variable that is declared in the next section.

Finally, create a directory called `Maps` to store the text files for defining the maps.

Now, it's time to go in-depth and be specific about implementing our grid graph. First, we implement all the functions for handling the graph, leaving space for your own text files, and, in the following section, we'll learn how to read `.map` files, which is an open format used by a lot of games:

1. Create the `GraphGrid` class, deriving from `Graph`:

```
using UnityEngine;
using System;
using System.Collections.Generic;
using System.IO;

public class GraphGrid : Graph
{
    public GameObject obstaclePrefab;
    public string mapName = "arena.map";
    public bool get8Vicinity = false;
```

```
        public float cellSize = 1f;
        [Range(0, Mathf.Infinity)]
        public float defaultCost = 1f;
        [Range(0, Mathf.Infinity)]
        public float maximumCost = Mathf.Infinity;
        string mapsDir = "Maps";
        int numCols;
        int numRows;
        GameObject[] vertexObjs;
        // this is necessary for
        // the advanced section of reading
        // from an example test file
        bool[,] mapVertices;
        // next steps
    }
```

2. Define the `GridToId` and `IdToGrid` functions for transforming a position in the grid into a vertex index, and vice versa:

```
    private int GridToId(int x, int y)
    {
        return Math.Max(numRows, numCols) * y + x;
    }

    private Vector2 IdToGrid(int id)
    {
        Vector2 location = Vector2.zero;
        location.y = Mathf.Floor(id / numCols);
        location.x = Mathf.Floor(id % numCols);
        return location;
    }
```

3. Define the `LoadMap` function for reading the text file:

```
    private void LoadMap(string filename)
    {
        // TODO
        // implement your grid-based
        // file-reading procedure here
        // using
        // vertices[i, j] for logical representation and
        // vertexObjs[i, j] for assigning new prefab instances
    }
```

4. Override the `LoadGraph` function:

```
public override void LoadGraph()
{
    LoadMap(mapName);
}
```

5. Override the `GetNearestVertex` function. This is the traditional way, without considering that the resulting vertex is an obstacle. In the following steps, we will learn how to do it better:

```
public override Vertex GetNearestVertex(Vector3 position)
{
    position.x = Mathf.Floor(position.x / cellSize);
    position.y = Mathf.Floor(position.z / cellSize);
    int col = (int)position.x;
    int row = (int)position.z;
    int id = GridToId(col, row);
    return vertices[id];
}
```

6. Override the `GetNearestVertex` function. It is based on the Breadth-First Search algorithm that we will learn about in-depth later in the chapter:

```
public override Vertex GetNearestVertex(Vector3 position)
{
    int col = (int)(position.x / cellSize);
    int row = (int)(position.z / cellSize);
    Vector2 p = new Vector2(col, row);
    // next steps
}
```

7. Define the list of explored positions (vertices) and the queue of the position to be explored:

```
List<Vector2> explored = new List<Vector2>();
Queue<Vector2> queue = new Queue<Vector2>();
queue.Enqueue(p);
```

8. Keep exploring while the queue still has elements to explore. Otherwise, return `null`:

```
do
{
    p = queue.Dequeue();
    col = (int)p.x;
    row = (int)p.y;
```

```
        int id = GridToId(col, row);
        // next steps
    } while (queue.Count != 0);
    return null;
```

9. Retrieve it immediately if it's a valid vertex:

```
if (mapVertices[row, col])
    return vertices[id];
```

10. Add the position to the list of explored, if it's not already there:

```
if (!explored.Contains(p))
{
    explored.Add(p);
    int i, j;
    // next step
}
```

11. Add all its valid neighbors to the queue, provided they are valid:

```
for (i = row - 1; i <= row + 1; i++)
{
    for (j = col - 1; j <= col + 1; j++)
    {
        if (i < 0 || j < 0)
            continue;
        if (j >= numCols || i >= numRows)
            continue;
        if (i == row && j == col)
            continue;
        queue.Enqueue(new Vector2(j, i));
    }
}
```

How it works...

The algorithm makes use of its private functions in order to adapt itself to the general functions derived from the parent's class, and it relies on simple mathematical functions to convert a two-dimensional vector position to a one-dimensional vector, or vertex index.

Grid representation

Vector representation
(general purpose)

```
 0  1  2
 3  4  5
 6  7  8
```

`0 1 2 3 4 5 6 7 8`

The LoadMap function needs to be implemented by you using your own map files, but, in the next section, we'll learn a way of implementing and reading certain kinds of text files containing maps based on grids. This will give you an idea of how to handle your files, and even use the same format for the commodity.

There's more...

We'll learn ways to implement the LoadMap function by using the .map file format as an example:

1. Define the function and create a StreamReader object for reading the file:

```
private void LoadMap(string filename)
{
    string path = Application.dataPath + "/" + mapsDir + "/" +
filename;
    try
    {
        StreamReader strmRdr = new StreamReader(path);
        using (strmRdr)
        {
            // next steps in here
        }
    }
    catch (Exception e)
    {
        Debug.LogException(e);
    }
}
```

2. Declare and initialize the necessary variables:

```
int j = 0;
int i = 0;
int id = 0;
string line;
Vector3 position = Vector3.zero;
Vector3 scale = Vector3.zero;
```

3. Read the header of the file containing its height and width:

```
line = strmRdr.ReadLine();// non-important line
line = strmRdr.ReadLine();// height
numRows = int.Parse(line.Split(' ')[1]);
line = strmRdr.ReadLine();// width
numCols = int.Parse(line.Split(' ')[1]);
line = strmRdr.ReadLine();// "map" line in file
```

4. Initialize the member variables, allocating memory at the same time:

```
vertices = new List<Vertex>(numRows * numCols);
neighbours = new List<List<Vertex>>(numRows * numCols);
costs = new List<List<float>>(numRows * numCols);
vertexObjs = new GameObject[numRows * numCols];
    mapVertices = new bool[numRows, numCols];
```

5. Declare the `for` loop for iterating over the characters in the following lines:

```
for (i = 0; i < numRows; i++)
{
    line = strmRdr.ReadLine();
    for (j = 0; j < numCols; j++)
    {
        // next steps in here
    }
}
```

6. Assign `true` or `false` to the logical representation depending on the character read:

```
bool isGround = true;
if (line[j] != '.')
    isGround = false;
mapVertices[i, j] = isGround;
```

7. Instantiate the proper prefab:

```
position.x = j * cellSize;
position.z = i * cellSize;
id = GridToId(j, i);
if (isGround)
    vertexObjs[id] = Instantiate(vertexPrefab, position,
Quaternion.identity) as GameObject;
else
    vertexObjs[id] = Instantiate(obstaclePrefab, position,
Quaternion.identity) as GameObject;
```

8. Assign the new game object as a child of the graph and clean up its name:

```
vertexObjs[id].name = vertexObjs[id].name.Replace("(Clone)",
id.ToString());
Vertex v = vertexObjs[id].AddComponent<Vertex>();
v.id = id;
vertices.Add(v);
neighbours.Add(new List<Vertex>());
costs.Add(new List<float>());
float y = vertexObjs[id].transform.localScale.y;
scale = new Vector3(cellSize, y, cellSize);
vertexObjs[id].transform.localScale = scale;
vertexObjs[id].transform.parent = gameObject.transform;
```

9. Create a pair of nested loops right after the previous loop, for setting up the neighbors for each vertex:

```
for (i = 0; i < numRows; i++)
{
    for (j = 0; j < numCols; j++)
    {
        SetNeighbours(j, i);
    }
}
```

10. Define the `SetNeighbours` function, called in the previous step:

```
protected void SetNeighbours(int x, int y, bool get8 = false)
{
    int col = x;
    int row = y;
    int i, j;
    int vertexId = GridToId(x, y);
    neighbours[vertexId] = new List<Vertex>();
```

```
        costs[vertexId] = new List<float>();
        Vector2[] pos = new Vector2[0];
        // next steps
    }
```

11. Compute the proper values when we need a vicinity of eight (top, bottom, right, left, and corners):

```
if (get8)
{
    pos = new Vector2[8];
    int c = 0;
    for (i = row - 1; i <= row + 1; i++)
    {
        for (j = col -1; j <= col; j++)
        {
            pos[c] = new Vector2(j, i);
            c++;
        }
    }
}
```

12. Set up everything for a vicinity of four (no corners):

```
else
{
    pos = new Vector2[4];
    pos[0] = new Vector2(col, row - 1);
    pos[1] = new Vector2(col - 1, row);
    pos[2] = new Vector2(col + 1, row);
    pos[3] = new Vector2(col, row + 1);
}
```

13. Add the neighbors to the lists. It's the same procedure as for the type of vicinity:

```
foreach (Vector2 p in pos)
{
    i = (int)p.y;
    j = (int)p.x;
    if (i < 0 || j < 0)
        continue;
    if (i >= numRows || j >= numCols)
        continue;
    if (i == row && j == col)
        continue;
    if (!mapVertices[i, j])
        continue;
```

```
int id = GridToId(j, i);
neighbours[vertexId].Add(vertices[id]);
costs[vertexId].Add(defaultCost);
}
```

See also

For further information about the map format used, and to get free maps from several acclaimed titles, please refer to the *Moving AI Lab's* website, led by Professor Sturtevant, available online at http://movingai.com/benchmarks/.

Representing the world with points of visibility

This is another widely-used technique for world representation based on points located throughout the valid area of navigation, be they manually placed or automated via scripting. We'll be using manually placed points connected automatically via scripting.

Getting ready

Just like the previous representation, it's important to have several things in order before continuing:

- Having the Edge class prepended to the Graph class in the same file
- Defining the GetEdges function in the Graph class
- Having the Vertex class

> The vertex objects in the scene must have a collider component attached to them, as well as the Vertex tag assigned. It's recommended that they are unitary Sphere primitives.

How to do it...

We'll be creating the graph representation class as well as a custom `Vertex` class:

1. Create the `VertexVisibility` class deriving from `Vertex`:

```csharp
using UnityEngine;
using System.Collections.Generic;

public class VertexVisibility : Vertex
{
    void Awake()
    {
        neighbours = new List<Edge>();
    }
}
```

2. Define the `FindNeighbours` function for automating the process of connecting vertices among them:

```csharp
public void FindNeighbours(List<Vertex> vertices)
{
    Collider c = gameObject.GetComponent<Collider>();
    c.enabled = false;
    Vector3 direction = Vector3.zero;
    Vector3 origin = transform.position;
    Vector3 target = Vector3.zero;
    RaycastHit[] hits;
    Ray ray;
    float distance = 0f;
    // next step
}
```

3. Go over each object and cast a ray to validate whether it's completely visible and add it to the list of neighbors:

```csharp
for (int i = 0; i < vertices.Count; i++)
{
    if (vertices[i] == this)
        continue;
    target = vertices[i].transform.position;
    direction = target - origin;
    distance = direction.magnitude;
    ray = new Ray(origin, direction);
    hits = Physics.RaycastAll(ray, distance);
    if (hits.Length == 1)
    {
```

```
        if (hits[0].collider.gameObject.tag.Equals("Vertex"))
        {
            Edge e = new Edge();
            e.cost = distance;
            GameObject go = hits[0].collider.gameObject;
            Vertex v = go.GetComponent<Vertex>();
            if (v != vertices[i])
                continue;
            e.vertex = v;
            neighbours.Add(e);
        }
    }
}
c.enabled = true;
```

4. **Create the** GraphVisibility **class:**

```
using UnityEngine;
using System.Collections.Generic;

public class GraphVisibility : Graph
{
    // next steps
}
```

5. **Build the** Load **function for making the connections between vertices:**

```
public override void Load()
{
    Vertex[] verts = GameObject.FindObjectsOfType<Vertex>();
    vertices = new List<Vertex>(verts);
    for (int i = 0; i < vertices.Count; i++)
    {
        VertexVisibility vv = vertices[i] as VertexVisibility;
        vv.id = i;
        vv.FindNeighbours(vertices);
    }
}
```

6. **Define the** GetNearesteVertex **function:**

```
public override Vertex GetNearestVertex(Vector3 position)
{
    Vertex vertex = null;
    float dist = Mathf.Infinity;
    float distNear = dist;
    Vector3 posVertex = Vector3.zero;
    for (int i = 0; i < vertices.Count; i++)
```

```
    {
        posVertex = vertices[i].transform.position;
        dist = Vector3.Distance(position, posVertex);
        if (dist < distNear)
        {
            distNear = dist;
            vertex = vertices[i];
        }
    }
    return vertex;
}
```

7. Define the `GetNeighbours` function:

```
public override Vertex[] GetNeighbours(Vertex v)
{
    List<Edge> edges = v.neighbours;
    Vertex[] ns = new Vertex[edges.Count];
    int i;
    for (i = 0; i < edges.Count; i++)
    {
        ns[i] = edges[i].vertex;
    }
    return ns;
}
```

8. Finally, override the `GetEdges` function:

```
public override Edge[] GetEdges(Vertex v)
{
    return vertices[v.id].neighbours.ToArray();
}
```

How it works...

The `GraphVisibility` parent class indexes every vertex on the scene and makes use of the `FindNeighbours` function on each one. This is in order to build the graph and make the connections without total user supervision, beyond placing the visibility points where the user sees fit. Also, the distance between two points is used to assign the cost to that corresponding edge.

There's more...

It's important to make points visible to one another in order for the graph to be connected. This approach is also suitable for building intelligent graphs considering stairs and cliffs; it just requires the moving of the `Load` function to an editor-friendly class in order to call it in edit mode, and then modifying or deleting the corresponding edges to make it work as intended.

Take a look at the previous recipe's *Getting ready* section so that you can better understand the starting point in case you feel you're missing something.

For further information about custom editors, editor scripting, and how to execute code in edit mode, please refer to the Unity documentation, available online at the following URLs:

- `http://docs.unity3d.com/ScriptReference/Editor.html`
- `http://docs.unity3d.com/ScriptReference/ExecuteInEditMode.html`
- `http://docs.unity3d.com/Manual/PlatformDependentCompilation.html`

Representing the world with a self-made navigation mesh

Sometimes, a custom navigation mesh is necessary for dealing with difficult situations such as different types of graphs, but placing the graph's vertices manually is troublesome because it requires a lot of time to cover large areas.

We will learn how to use a model's mesh in order to generate a navigation mesh based on its triangles' centroids as vertices, and then leverage the heavy lifting we learned from the previous recipe.

Getting ready

This recipe requires some knowledge of custom editor scripting and an understanding of implementing the points of visibility graph representation. Also, it is worth mentioning that the script instantiates a `CustomNavMesh` game object automatically in the scene and it requires a prefab to be assigned, just like any other graph representation.

Finally, it's important to create the following class, deriving from `GraphVisibility`:

```
using UnityEngine;
using System.Collections;
using System.Collections.Generic;

public class CustomNavMesh : GraphVisibility
{
    public override void Start()
    {
        instIdToId = new Dictionary<int, int>();
    }
}
```

How to do it...

We will create an editor window for easily handling the automation process without weighing down the graph's `Start` function, thereby delaying the scene loading:

1. Create the `CustomNavMeshWindow` class and place it in a directory called Editor:

   ```
   using UnityEngine;
   using UnityEditor;
   using System.Collections;
   using System.Collections.Generic;

   public class CustomNavMeshWindow : EditorWindow
   {
       // next steps here
   }
   ```

2. Add the attributes to the editor window:

   ```
   static bool isEnabled = false;
   static GameObject graphObj;
   static CustomNavMesh graph;
   static CustomNavMeshWindow window;
   static GameObject graphVertex;
   ```

3. Implement the function for initializing and showing the window:

   ```
   [MenuItem("UAIPC/Ch02/CustomNavMeshWindow")]
   static void Init()
   {
       window = EditorWindow.GetWindow<CustomNavMeshWindow>();
       window.title = "CustomNavMeshWindow";
   ```

```
SceneView.onSceneGUIDelegate += OnScene;
graphObj = GameObject.Find("CustomNavMesh");
if (graphObj == null)
{
    graphObj = new GameObject("CustomNavMesh");
    graphObj.AddComponent<CustomNavMesh>();
    graph = graphObj.GetComponent<CustomNavMesh>();
}
else
{
    graph = graphObj.GetComponent<CustomNavMesh>();
    if (graph == null)
        graphObj.AddComponent<CustomNavMesh>();
    graph = graphObj.GetComponent<CustomNavMesh>();
}
}
```

4. Define the `OnDestroy` function:

```
void OnDestroy()
{
    SceneView.onSceneGUIDelegate -= OnScene;
}
```

5. Implement the `OnGUI` function for drawing the window's interior:

```
void OnGUI()
{
    isEnabled = EditorGUILayout.Toggle("Enable Mesh Picking",
isEnabled);
    if (GUILayout.Button("Build Edges"))
    {
        if (graph != null)
            graph.LoadGraph();
    }
}
```

6. Implement the first half of the `OnScene` function for handling the left-click on the scene window:

```
private static void OnScene(SceneView sceneView)
{
    if (!isEnabled)
        return;
    if (Event.current.type == EventType.MouseDown)
    {
        graphVertex = graph.vertexPrefab;
        if (graphVertex == null)
```

```
        {
            Debug.LogError("No Vertex Prefab assigned");
            return;
        }
        Event e = Event.current;
        Ray ray =
HandleUtility.GUIPointToWorldRay(e.mousePosition);
        RaycastHit hit;
        GameObject newV;
        // next step
    }
}
```

7. Implement the second half for implementing the behavior when clicking on the mesh:

```
if (Physics.Raycast(ray, out hit))
{
    GameObject obj = hit.collider.gameObject;
    Mesh mesh = obj.GetComponent<MeshFilter>().sharedMesh;
    Vector3 pos;
    int i;
    for (i = 0; i < mesh.triangles.Length; i += 3)
    {
        int i0 = mesh.triangles[i];
        int i1 = mesh.triangles[i + 1];
        int i2 = mesh.triangles[i + 2];
        pos = mesh.vertices[i0];
        pos += mesh.vertices[i1];
        pos += mesh.vertices[i2];
        pos /= 3;
        newV = (GameObject)Instantiate(graphVertex, pos,
Quaternion.identity);
        newV.transform.Translate(obj.transform.position);
        newV.transform.parent = graphObj.transform;
        graphObj.transform.parent = obj.transform;
    }
}
```

How it works...

We create a custom editor window and set up the `OnScene` delegate function for handling events on the scene window. Also, we are capable of creating the graph nodes by traversing the mesh vertex arrays, computing each triangle's centroid. Finally, we make use of the graph's `LoadGraph` function in order to compute neighbors.

Finding your way out of a maze with DFS

The **Depth-First Search** (**DFS**) algorithm is a path-finding technique suitable for low-memory devices. Another common use is to build mazes with some minor modifications to the list of nodes visited and discovered, but the main algorithm stays just the same.

Getting ready

This is a high-level algorithm that relies on each graph's implementation of the main functions (`build`, `init`, and so on), so that the algorithm is implemented in the `Graph` class.

It is important to take a moment and verify when the recipe is manipulating actual objects, or vertex IDs.

How to do it...

Even though this recipe is only defining a function, please take into consideration the comments in the code for better understanding of the implementation and code flow:

1. Declare the `GetPathDFS` function:

```
public List<Vertex> GetPathDFS(GameObject srcObj, GameObject
dstObj)
{
    // next steps
}
```

2. Establish whether input objects are `null`:

```
if (srcObj == null || dstObj == null)
    return new List<Vertex>();
```

3. Declare and initialize the variables we need for the algorithm:

```
Vertex src = GetNearestVertex(srcObj.transform.position);
Vertex dst = GetNearestVertex(dstObj.transform.position);
Vertex[] neighbours;
Vertex v;
int[] previous = new int[vertices.Count];
for (int i = 0; i < previous.Length; i++)
    previous[i] = -1;
previous[src.id] = src.id;
Stack<Vertex> s = new Stack<Vertex>();
s.Push(src);
```

4. Implement the DFS algorithm for finding a path:

```
while (s.Count != 0)
{
    v = s.Pop();
    if (ReferenceEquals(v, dst))
    {
        return BuildPath(src.id, v.id, ref previous);
    }

    neighbours = GetNeighbours(v);
    foreach (Vertex n in neighbours)
    {
        if (previous[n.id] != -1)
            continue;
        previous[n.id] = v.id;
        s.Push(n);
    }
}
```

How it works...

The algorithm is based on the iterative version of DFS. It is also based on the in-order traversing of a graph and the LIFO philosophy of using a stack for visiting nodes and adding discovered ones.

There's more...

We called the BuildPath function, but we haven't implemented it yet. It is important to note that this function is called by almost every other path-finding algorithm in this chapter; that's why it's not part of the main recipe.

This is the code for the `BuildPath` method:

```
private List<Vertex> BuildPath(int srcId, int dstId, ref int[] prevList)
{
    List<Vertex> path = new List<Vertex>();
    int prev = dstId;
    do
    {
        path.Add(vertices[prev]);
        prev = prevList[prev];
    } while (prev != srcId);
    return path;
}
```

Finding the shortest path in a grid with BFS

The **Breadth-First Search** (**BFS**) algorithm is just another basic technique for graph traversal and is aimed at getting the shortest path in the fewest steps possible, with the trade-off of being expensive in memory; thus, it is aimed especially at games for high-end consoles and computers.

Getting ready

This is a high-level algorithm that relies on each graph's implementation of the general functions, so the algorithm is implemented in the `Graph` class.

How to do it...

Even though this recipe is only defining a function, please take into consideration the comments in the code for better understanding of the implementation and code flow:

1. Declare the `GetPathBFS` function:

```
public List<Vertex> GetPathBFS(GameObject srcObj, GameObject
dstObj)
{
    if (srcObj == null || dstObj == null)
        return new List<Vertex>();
    // next steps
}
```

2. Declare and initialize the variables we need for the algorithm:

```
Vertex[] neighbours;
Queue<Vertex> q = new Queue<Vertex>();
Vertex src = GetNearestVertex(srcObj.transform.position);
Vertex dst = GetNearestVertex(dstObj.transform.position);
Vertex v;
int[] previous = new int[vertices.Count];
for (int i = 0; i < previous.Length; i++)
    previous[i] = -1;
previous[src.id] = src.id;
q.Enqueue(src);
```

3. Implement the BFS algorithm for finding a path:

```
while (q.Count != 0)
{
    v = q.Dequeue();
    if (ReferenceEquals(v, dst))
    {
        return BuildPath(src.id, v.id, ref previous);
    }

    neighbours = GetNeighbours(v);
    foreach (Vertex n in neighbours)
    {
        if (previous[n.id] != -1)
            continue;
        previous[n.id] = v.id;
        q.Enqueue(n);
    }
}
return new List<Vertex>();
```

How it works...

The BFS algorithm is similar to the DFS algorithm because it's based on the same in-order traversing of a graph but, instead of a stack such as DFS, BFS uses a queue for visiting the discovered nodes.

There's more...

In case you haven't noticed, we didn't implement the `BuildPath` method. This is because we talked about it at the end of the recipe in `Chapter 2`, *Navigation*, in the recipe *Finding your way out of a maze with DFS*.

Finding the shortest path with Dijkstra

Dijkstra's algorithm was initially designed to solve the single-source shortest path problem for a graph. Thus, the algorithm finds the lowest-cost route to everywhere from a single point. We will learn how to make use of it given two different approaches.

Getting ready

The first thing to do is to import the binary heap class from the **Game Programming Wiki (GPWiki)** into our project, given that neither the .Net framework nor Mono have a defined structure for handling binary heaps or priority queues.

The source file is already in the book's online repository service provider as it is no longer available online.

How to do it...

We will learn how to implement the Dijkstra algorithm using the same number of parameters as the other algorithms, and then explain how to modify it to make maximum use of it according to its original purpose:

1. Define the `GetPathDijkstra` function with its internal variables:

```
public List<Vertex> GetPathDijkstra(GameObject srcObj, GameObject
dstObj)
{
    if (srcObj == null || dstObj == null)
        return new List<Vertex>();
    Vertex src = GetNearestVertex(srcObj.transform.position);
    Vertex dst = GetNearestVertex(dstObj.transform.position);
    GPWiki.BinaryHeap<Edge> frontier = new
GPWiki.BinaryHeap<Edge>();
    Edge[] edges;
    Edge node, child;
```

```
        int size = vertices.Count;
        float[] distValue = new float[size];
        int[] previous = new int[size];

        // next steps
    }
```

2. Add the source node to the heap (working as a priority queue) and assign a distance value of infinity to all of them but the source node:

```
node = new Edge(src, 0);
frontier.Add(node);
distValue[src.id] = 0;
previous[src.id] = src.id;
for (int i = 0; i < size; i++)
{
    if (i == src.id)
        continue;
    distValue[i] = Mathf.Infinity;
    previous[i] = -1;
}
```

3. Define a loop to iterate while the queue is not empty:

```
while (frontier.Count != 0)
{
    node = frontier.Remove();
    int nodeId = node.vertex.id;
    // next steps
}
return new List<Vertex>();
```

4. Code the procedure when arriving at the destination:

```
if (ReferenceEquals(node.vertex, dst))
{
    return BuildPath(src.id, node.vertex.id, ref previous);
}
```

5. Otherwise, process the visited nodes and add its neighbors to the queue, and return the path (not empty if there is a path from the source to the destination vertex):

```
edges = GetEdges(node.vertex);
foreach (Edge e in edges)
{
    int eId = e.vertex.id;
    if (previous[eId] != -1)
```

```
        continue;
    float cost = distValue[nodeId] + e.cost;
    if (cost < distValue[e.vertex.id])
    {
        distValue[eId] = cost;
        previous[eId] = nodeId;
        frontier.Remove(e);
        child = new Edge(e.vertex, cost);
        frontier.Add(child);
    }
}
```

How it works...

Dijkstra's algorithm works in a similar way to BFS, but considers non-negative edge costs in order to build the best route from the source vertex to every other vertex. That's why we have an array for storing what the previous vertex is.

There's more...

We will learn how to modify the current Dijkstra algorithm in order to approach the problem using pre-processing techniques and optimizing the path-finding time. It can be seen as three big steps—modifying the main algorithm, creating the pre-processing function (handy in editor mode, for example), and, finally, defining the path retrieval function:

1. Modify the main function's signature:

    ```
    public int[] Dijkstra(GameObject srcObj)
    ```

2. Change the returning value:

    ```
    return previous;
    ```

3. Remove the lines from step 4 of the *How to do it* section:

    ```
    if (ReferenceEquals(node.vertex, dst))
    {
        return BuildPath(src.id, node.vertex.id, ref previous);
    }
    ```

    Also, delete the following line at the beginning:

    ```
    Vertex dst = GetNearestVertex(dstObj.transform.position);
    ```

4. Create a new member value for the `Graph` class:

```
List<int[]> routes = new List<int[]>();
```

5. Define the pre-processing function, called `DijkstraProcessing`:

```
public void DijkstraProcessing()
{
    int size = GetSize();
    for (int i = 0; i < size; i++)
    {
        GameObject go = vertices[i].gameObject;
        routes.add(Dijkstra(go));
    }
}
```

6. Implement a new `GetPathDijkstra` function for path retrieval:

```
public List<Vertex> GetPathDijkstra(GameObject srcObj, GameObject
dstObj)
{
    List<Vertex> path = new List<Vertex>();
    Vertex src = GetNearestVertex(srcObj);
    Vertex dst = GetNearestVertex(dstObj);
    return BuildPath(src.id, dst.id, ref routes[dst.id]);
}
```

In case you haven't noticed, we didn't implement the `BuildPath` method. This is because we talked about it at the end of `Chapter 2`, *Navigation,* in the recipe *Finding your way out of a maze with DFS.*

Finding the best-promising path with A*

The A* algorithm is probably the most widely-used technique for path finding given its implementation simplicity, efficiency, and because it has room for optimization. It's no coincidence that there are several algorithms based on it. At the same time, A* shares several roots with Dijkstra's algorithm, so you'll find similarities in their implementations.

Getting ready

Just like Dijkstra's algorithm, this recipe uses the binary heap extracted from the GPWiki. Also, it is important to understand what delegates are and how they work. Finally, we are entering into the world of informed search; that means that we need to understand what a heuristic is and what it is for.

In a nutshell, for the purpose of this recipe, a heuristic is a function for calculating the approximate cost between two vertices in order to compare them to other alternatives and take the minimum-cost choice.

We need to make small changes to the `Graph` class:

1. Define a member variable as a `delegate`:

   ```
   public delegate float Heuristic(Vertex a, Vertex b);
   ```

2. Implement a Euclidean distance member function to use it as a default heuristic:

   ```
   public float EuclidDist(Vertex a, Vertex b)
   {
       Vector3 posA = a.transform.position;
       Vector3 posB = b.transform.position;
       return  Vector3.Distance(posA, posB);
   }
   ```

3. Implement a Manhattan distance function to use as a different heuristic. It will help us in comparing results using different heuristics:

   ```
   public float ManhattanDist(Vertex a, Vertex b)
   {
       Vector3 posA = a.transform.position;
       Vector3 posB = b.transform.position;
       return Mathf.Abs(posA.x - posB.x) + Mathf.Abs(posA.y - posB.y);
   }
   ```

How to do it...

Even though this recipe covers defining a function, please take into consideration the comments in the code for better understanding of the implementation and code flow:

1. Define the `GetPathAstar` function, along with its member variables:

   ```
   public List<Vertex> GetPathAstar(GameObject srcObj, GameObject
   dstObj, Heuristic h = null)
   ```

```
    {
        if (srcObj == null || dstObj == null)
            return new List<Vertex>();
        if (ReferenceEquals(h, null))
            h = EuclidDist;

        Vertex src = GetNearestVertex(srcObj.transform.position);
        Vertex dst = GetNearestVertex(dstObj.transform.position);
        GPWiki.BinaryHeap<Edge> frontier = new
GPWiki.BinaryHeap<Edge>();
        Edge[] edges;
        Edge node, child;
        int size = vertices.Count;
        float[] distValue = new float[size];
        int[] previous = new int[size];
        // next steps
    }
```

2. Add the source node to the heap (working as a priority queue) and assign a distance value of infinity to all of them bar the source node:

```
node = new Edge(src, 0);
frontier.Add(node);
distValue[src.id] = 0;
previous[src.id] = src.id;
for (int i = 0; i < size; i++)
{
    if (i == src.id)
        continue;
    distValue[i] = Mathf.Infinity;
    previous[i] = -1;
}
```

3. Declare the loop for traversing the graph:

```
while (frontier.Count != 0)
{
    // next steps
}
return new List<Vertex>();
```

4. Implement the conditions for returning a path when necessary:

```
node = frontier.Remove();
int nodeId = node.vertex.id;
if (ReferenceEquals(node.vertex, dst))
```

```
{
    return BuildPath(src.id, node.vertex.id, ref previous);
}
```

5. Get the vertex's neighbors (also called successors in some textbooks):

```
edges = GetEdges(node.vertex);
```

6. Traverse the neighbors for computing the `cost` function:

```
foreach (Edge e in edges)
{
    int eId = e.vertex.id;
    if (previous[eId] != -1)
        continue;
    float cost = distValue[nodeId] + e.cost;
    // key point
    cost += h(node.vertex, e.vertex);
    // next step
}
```

7. Expand the list of explored nodes (`frontier`) and update the costs, if necessary:

```
if (cost < distValue[e.vertex.id])
{
    distValue[eId] = cost;
    previous[eId] = nodeId;
    frontier.Remove(e);
    child = new Edge(e.vertex, cost);
    frontier.Add(child);
}
```

How it works...

A* works in a similar fashion to Dijkstra's algorithm. However, instead of choosing the real lowest-cost node from all the possible options, it chooses the most promising one based on a given heuristic, and goes that way. In our case, the default heuristic is based solely on the Euclidean distance between two vertices with the option of using Manhattan distance.

There's more...

You are welcome to play with different heuristic functions depending on the game and context, and the following is an example of how to do so.

Define a heuristic function in the `Graph` class:

```
public float Heuristic(Vertex a, Vertex b)
{
    float estimation = 0f;
    // your logic here
    return estimation;
}
```

The important thing here is that the heuristic we develop is both *admissible* and *consistent*. For more theoretical insights about these topics, please refer to *Artificial Intelligence: A Modern Approach*, by Russel and Norvig.

In case you haven't noticed, we didn't implement the `BuildPath` method. This is because we talked about it at the end of `Chapter 2`, *Navigation*, in the recipe *Finding your way out of a maze with DFS*.

See also

In this chapter, please refer to the following recipes:

- *Finding your way out of a maze with DFS*

- *Finding the shortest path with Dijsktra*

For further information about Delegates, please refer to the official documentation available online at `https://unity3d.com/learn/tutorials/modules/intermediate/scripting/delegates`.

Improving A* for memory – IDA*

IDA* is a variant of an algorithm called Iterative Deepening Depth-First Search. Its memory usage is lower than A* because it doesn't make use of data structures to store the looked-up and explored nodes.

Getting ready

For this recipe, it is important to have some understanding of how recursion works.

How to do it...

This is a long recipe that can be regarded as a big two-step process: creating the main function and an internal recursive one. Please take into consideration the comments in the code for better understanding of the implementation and code flow:

1. Let's start by defining the main function, `GetPathIDAstar`:

```
public List<Vertex> GetPathIDAstar(GameObject srcObj, GameObject
dstObj, Heuristic h = null)
{
    if (srcObj == null || dstObj == null)
        return new List<Vertex>();
    if (ReferenceEquals(h, null))
        h = EuclidDist;
    // next steps;
}
```

2. Declare and compute the variables to use alongside the algorithm:

```
List<Vertex> path = new List<Vertex>();
Vertex src = GetNearestVertex(srcObj.transform.position);
Vertex dst = GetNearestVertex(dstObj.transform.position);
Vertex goal = null;
bool[] visited = new bool[vertices.Count];
for (int i = 0; i < visited.Length; i++)
visited[i] = false;
visited[src.id] = true;
```

3. Implement the algorithm's loop:

```
float bound = h(src, dst);
while (bound < Mathf.Infinity)
{
    bound = RecursiveIDAstar(src, dst, bound, h, ref goal, ref
visited);
}
if (ReferenceEquals(goal, null))
    return path;
return BuildPath(goal);
```

4. Now it's time to build the recursive internal function:

```
private float RecursiveIDAstar(
        Vertex v,
        Vertex dst,
        float bound,
        Heuristic h,
```

```
            ref Vertex goal,
            ref bool[] visited)
{
    // next steps
}
```

5. Prepare everything to start the recursion:

```
// base case
if (ReferenceEquals(v, dst))
    return Mathf.Infinity;
Edge[] edges = GetEdges(v);
if (edges.Length == 0)
    return Mathf.Infinity;
```

6. Apply the recursion for each neighbor:

```
// recursive case
float fn = Mathf.Infinity;
foreach (Edge e in edges)
{
    int eId = e.vertex.id;
    if (visited[eId])
        continue;
    visited[eId] = true;
    e.vertex.prev = v;
    float f = h(v, dst);
    float b;
    if (f <= bound)
    {
        b = RecursiveIDAstar(e.vertex, dst, bound, h, ref goal, ref
visited);
        fn = Mathf.Min(f, b);
    }
    else
        fn = Mathf.Min(fn, f);
}
```

7. Return a value based on the recursion result:

```
return fn;
```

How it works...

As you can see, the algorithm is very similar to that of the recursive version of DFS, but uses the principle of making decisions on top of a heuristic from A*. The main function is responsible for starting the recursion and building the resulting path. The recursive function is the one responsible for traversing the graph, looking for the destination node.

There's more...

This time, we will need to implement a different `BuildPath` function, in case you have followed along with the previous path-finding recipes. Otherwise, we will need to implement this method, which we haven't defined yet:

```
private List<Vertex> BuildPath(Vertex v)
{
    List<Vertex> path = new List<Vertex>();
    while (!ReferenceEquals(v, null))
    {
        path.Add(v);
        v = v.prev;
    }
    return path;
}
```

Planning navigation in several frames – time-sliced search

When dealing with large graphs, computing paths can take a lot of time, even driving the game to a halt for a couple of seconds. This could lead to ruining the overall experience, to say the least. Luckily enough, there are methods for avoiding that.

 This recipe is built on top of the principles of using coroutines as a method for keeping the game running smoothly while finding a path in the background; some knowledge of coroutines is required.

Getting ready

We'll learn how to implement path-finding techniques using coroutines by refactoring the A* algorithm learned previously, but we will handle its signature as a different function.

How to do it...

Even though this recipe is only for defining a function, please take into consideration the comments in the code for a better understanding of the implementation and code flow:

1. Modify the `Graph` class and add a couple of member variables, one for storing the path and the other for knowing whether the coroutine has finished:

```
public List<Vertex> path;
public bool isFinished;
```

2. Declare the member function:

```
public IEnumerator GetPathInFrames(GameObject srcObj, GameObject
dstObj, Heuristic h = null)
{
    //next steps
}
```

3. Include the following member variables at the beginning:

```
isFinished = false;
path = new List<Vertex>();
if (srcObj == null || dstObj == null)
{
    path = new List<Vertex>();
    isFinished = true;
    yield break;
}
```

4. Modify the loop for traversing the graph:

```
while (frontier.Count != 0)
{
    // changes over A*
    yield return null;
    ////////////////////////////
    node = frontier.Remove();
```

5. Also, include the other path-retrieval validations:

```
if (ReferenceEquals(node.vertex, dst))
{
    // changes over A*
    path = BuildPath(src.id, node.vertex.id, ref previous);
    break;
    /////////////////////////////
}
```

6. Finally, reset the proper values and return control at the end of the function, after closing the main loop:

```
isFinished = true;
yield break;
```

How it works...

The `yield return null` statement inside the main loop works as a flag for delivering control to the higher-level functions, thus computing each new loop in each new frame using Unity's internal multitasking system.

See also

- The *Finding the best-promising path with A** recipe

For further information about coroutines and more examples, please refer to the official documentation available online at the following URLs:

- http://docs.unity3d.com/Manual/Coroutines.html
- https://unity3d.com/learn/tutorials/modules/intermediate/scripting/coroutines

Smoothing a path

When dealing with regular-size vertices on a graph, such as grids, it's pretty common to see some kind of *robotic* movement from the agents in the game. Depending on the type of game we're developing, this could be avoided using path-smoothing techniques, such as the one we're about to learn:

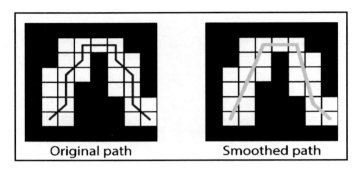

Original path   Smoothed path

Getting ready

Let's define a new tag in the Unity editor called `Wall` and assign it to every object in the scene that is intended to work as a wall or obstacle in the navigation.

How to do it...

This is an easy, yet powerful, function:

1. Define the `Smooth` function:

```
public List<Vertex> Smooth(List<Vertex> path)
{
    // next steps here
}
```

2. Check whether it is worth computing a new path:

```
List<Vertex> newPath = new List<Vertex>();
if (path.Count == 0)
    return newPath;
if (path.Count < 3)
    return path;
```

3. Implement the loops for traversing the list and building the new path:

```
newPath.Add(path[0]);
int i, j;
for (i = 0; i < path.Count - 1;)
{
    for (j = i + 1; j < path.Count; j++)
    {
        // next steps here
    }
    i = j - 1;
    newPath.Add(path[i]);
}
return newPath;
```

4. Declare and compute the variables to be used by the ray casting function:

```
Vector3 origin = path[i].transform.position;
Vector3 destination = path[j].transform.position;
Vector3 direction = destination - origin;
float distance = direction.magnitude;
bool isWall = false;
direction.Normalize();
```

5. Cast a ray from the current starting node to the next one:

```
Ray ray = new Ray(origin, direction);
RaycastHit[] hits;
hits = Physics.RaycastAll(ray, distance);
```

6. Check whether there is a wall and break the loop accordingly:

```
foreach (RaycastHit hit in hits)
{
    string tag = hit.collider.gameObject.tag;
    if (tag.Equals("Wall"))
    {
        isWall = true;
        break;
    }
}
if (isWall)
    break;
```

How it works...

We create a new path, taking the initial node as a starting point, and apply ray casting to the next node in the path until we get a collision with a wall between our current node and the target node. When that happens, we take the last clear node, put it in the new path, and set it as the current node to start casting rays again. The process continues until there are no nodes left to check and the current node is the target node. That way, we build a more intuitive path.

3
Decision Making

In this chapter, we will cover the following recipes:

- Choosing through a decision tree
- Implementing a finite-state machine
- Improving FSMs: hierarchical finite-state machines
- Implementing behavior trees
- Working with fuzzy logic
- Making decisions with goal-oriented behaviors
- Implementing a blackboard architecture
- Experimenting with Unity's animation state machine

Introduction

Making decisions or changing the game flow according to the game's state could get really messy if we rely only on simple control structures. That's why we will learn different decision-making techniques that are flexible enough to adapt to different types of games, and robust enough to let us build modular decision-making systems.

The techniques covered in the chapter are mostly related to trees, automata, and matrices. Also, certain topics require a good understanding of how recursion, inheritance, and polymorphism work, so it is important that we review those topics if required.

Choosing through a decision tree

One of the simplest mechanisms for tackling decision-making problems is decision trees, because they are fast and easy to grasp and implement. As a consequence, it's one of the most widely-used techniques today; it is extensively used in other character-controlled scopes such as animations.

Getting ready

This recipe requires a good understanding of recursion and inheritance, as we will constantly be implementing and calling virtual functions throughout the sections.

How to do it...

This recipe requires a lot of attention due to the number of files that we will need to handle. Overall, we will create a parent class `DecisionTreeNode`, from which we will derive the other ones. Finally, we will learn how to implement a couple of standard decision nodes:

1. First, create the `DecisionTreeNode` parent class, as shown in the following code:

```
using UnityEngine;
using System.Collections;
public class DecisionTreeNode : MonoBehaviour
{
    public virtual DecisionTreeNode MakeDecision()
    {
        return null;
    }
}
```

2. Next, create the `Decision` pseudo-abstract class, deriving from the parent class, `DecisionTreeNode`, as demonstrated in the following code:

```
using UnityEngine;
using System.Collections;
public class Decision : DecisionTreeNode
{
    public Action nodeTrue;
    public Action nodeFalse;

    public virtual Action GetBranch()
    {
        return null;
    }
}
```

3. Then, we need to define the `Action` pseudo-abstract class, as shown in the following code:

```
using UnityEngine;
using System.Collections;
public class Action : DecisionTreeNode
{
    public bool activated = false;

    public override DecisionTreeNode MakeDecision()
    {
        return this;
    }
}
```

4. We then implement the `LateUpdate` virtual function, as shown in the following code:

```
public virtual void LateUpdate()
{
    if (!activated)
        return;
    // Implement your behaviors here
}
```

5. Next, we create the final class, `DecisionTree`, as shown in the following code:

```
using UnityEngine;
using System.Collections;
public class DecisionTree : DecisionTreeNode
{
    public DecisionTreeNode root;
    private Action actionNew;
    private Action actionOld;
}
```

6. We then override the `MakeDecision` function with the following code:

```
public override DecisionTreeNode MakeDecision()
{
    return root.MakeDecision();
}
```

7. Finally, we then implement the `Update` function, as demonstrated in the following code:

```
void Update()
{
    actionNew.activated = false;
    actionOld = actionNew;
    actionNew = root.MakeDecision() as Action;
    if (actionNew == null)
        actionNew = actionOld;
    actionNew.activated = true;
}
```

How it works...

Decision nodes choose which path to take, calling the `MakeDecision` function recursively. It is worth mentioning that branches must be decisions, and leaves must be actions. Also, we should be careful not to create cycles within the tree:

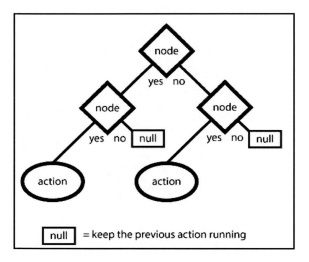

There's more...

We can create custom decisions and actions starting from the pseudo-abstract classes we've already created; for example, a decision on whether to attack or run away from the player.

The following code snippet demonstrates the custom Boolean decision:

```
using UnityEngine;
using System.Collections;

public class DecisionBool : Decision
{
    public bool valueDecision;
    public bool valueTest;

    public override Action GetBranch()
    {
        if (valueTest == valueDecision)
            return nodeTrue;
        return nodeFalse;
    }
}
```

Implementing a finite-state machine

Another interesting, yet easy-to-implement, technique is the **finite-state machine** (**FSM**). Finite-state machines move us to change the train of thought from what it was in the previous recipe. FSMs are great when our train of thought is more event-oriented, and we think in terms of holding a behavior until a condition is met, changing to another.

Getting ready

This is a technique mostly based on the behavior of automata, and will lay the foundations for the next recipe, which is an improved version of the current one.

How to do it...

This recipe is broken down into implementing three classes from the ground up. Don't worry, everything will make sense by the final step:

1. First, we'll implement the `Condition` class, as shown in the following code:

    ```
    public class Condition
    {
        public virtual bool Test()
        {
            return false;
        }
    }
    ```

2. Next, we're going to define the `Transition` class, as demonstrated in the following code:

    ```
    public class Transition
    {
        public Condition condition;
        public State target;
    }
    ```

3. We then need to define the `State` class, which is shown in the following code:

    ```
    using UnityEngine;
    using System.Collections.Generic;

    public class State : MonoBehaviour
    {
        public List<Transition> transitions;
    }
    ```

4. Then, we implement the `Awake` function, as you'll see in the following code:

    ```
    public virtual void Awake()
    {
        transitions = new List<Transition>();
        // TO-DO
        // setup your transitions here
    }
    ```

5. The next stage is to define the initialization function, as shown in the following code:

```
public virtual void OnEnable()
{
    // TO-DO
    // develop state's initialization here
}
```

6. We then define the finalization function, as you'll see in the following code:

```
public virtual void OnDisable()
{
    // TO-DO
    // develop state's finalization here
}
```

7. Next, we define the function for developing the proper behavior for the state, as shown in the following code:

```
public virtual void Update()
{
    // TO-DO
    // develop behaviour here
}
```

8. Finally, we implement the function for deciding if and which state is next enabled, as shown in the following code:

```
public void LateUpdate()
{
    foreach (Transition t in transitions)
    {
        if (t.condition.Test())
        {
            t.target.enabled = true;
            this.enabled = false;
            return;
        }
    }
}
```

How it works...

Each state is a `MonoBehaviour` script that is enabled or disabled according to the transitions it comes from. We take advantage of the `LateUpdate` function in order not to change the usual train of thought when developing behaviors, and we use it to check if it is time to transition to a different state. It is important to disable every state in the game object, apart from the initial one.

The following diagram shows the graphical representation for a finite-state machine.

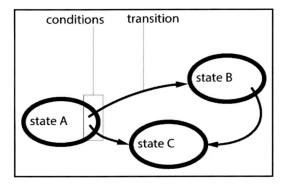

A finite-state machine representation

There's more...

In order to illustrate how to develop child classes deriving from the `Condition` function, let's take a look at a couple of examples; one that is aimed at validating a value in a range, the other at being a logic comparer between two conditions:

The code for `ConditionFloat` is as follows:

```
using UnityEngine;
using System.Collections;

public class ConditionFloat : Condition
{
    public float valueMin;
    public float valueMax;
    public float valueTest;

    public override bool Test()
    {
```

```
        if (valueMax >= valueTest && valueTest >= valueMin)
            return true;
        return false;
    }
}
```

The following code is an example of code for `ConditionAnd`:

```
using UnityEngine;
using System.Collections;

public class ConditionAnd : Condition
{
    public Condition conditionA;
    public Condition conditionB;

    public override bool Test()
    {
        if (conditionA.Test() && conditionB.Test())
            return true;
        return false;
    }
}
```

Improving FSMs: hierarchical finite-state machines

Finite-state machines can be improved in terms of having different layers or hierarchies. The principles are the same, but states are able to have their own internal finite-state machine, making them more flexible and scalable.

Getting ready

This recipe is based on top of the previous recipe, so it is important that we first grasp and understand how the finite-state machine recipe works.

How to do it...

We will create a state that is capable of holding internal states, in order to develop multilevel hierarchical state machines:

1. First, let's create the `StateHighLevel` class deriving from `State`, as shown in the following code:

```
using UnityEngine;
using System.Collections;
using System.Collections.Generic;

public class StateHighLevel : State
{
}
```

2. Next, add the new member variables to control the internal states, as demonstrated in the following code:

```
public List<State> states;
public State stateInitial;
protected State stateCurrent;
```

3. Then, we override the initialization function, as shown in the following code:

```
public override void OnEnable()
{
    if (stateCurrent == null)
        stateCurrent = stateInitial;
    stateCurrent.enabled = true;
}
```

4. Finally, we override the finalization function, as shown in the following code:

```
public override void OnDisable()
{
    base.OnDisable();
    stateCurrent.enabled = false;
    foreach (State s in states)
    {
        s.enabled = false;
    }
}
```

How it works...

The high-level state class allows us to activate the internal FSMs when it is enabled, and recursively disables its internal states when disabled. The working principle stays the same, thanks to the list of states and the way the parent class resolves the transitioning process.

See also

For further details, please refer to the following recipe in this chapter:

- *Implementing a finite-state machine* recipe.

Implementing behavior trees

Behavior trees can be seen as a synthesis of a number of other artificial intelligence techniques, such as finite-state machines, planning, and decision trees. In fact, they share some resemblance to FSMs, but instead of states, we think in terms of actions spanned across a tree structure.

Getting ready

This recipe requires us to understand coroutines.

How to do it...

Just like decisions trees, we will create three pseudo-abstract classes for handling the process:

1. First, let's create the `Task` base class, as shown in the following code:

   ```
   using UnityEngine;
   using System.Collections;
   using System.Collections.Generic;

   public class Task : MonoBehaviour
   {
   ```

```
        public List<Task> children;
        protected bool result = false;
        protected bool isFinished = false;
    }
```

2. Next, we're going to implement the finalization function, as shown in the following code:

```
public virtual void SetResult(bool r)
{
    result = r;
    isFinished = true;
}
```

3. We then implement the function for creating behaviors, as follows:

```
public virtual IEnumerator Run()
{
    SetResult(true);
    yield break;
}
```

4. We then implement the general function for starting behaviors, as demonstrated in the following code:

```
public virtual IEnumerator RunTask()
{
    yield return StartCoroutine(Run());
}
```

5. Next, we create the `ConditionBT` class, as shown in the following code:

```
using UnityEngine;
using System.Collections;

public class ConditionBT : Task
{
    public override IEnumerator Run()
    {
        isFinished = false;
        bool r = false;
        // implement your behaviour here
        // define result (r) whether true or false
        //---------
        SetResult(r);
        yield break;
    }
}
```

6. Then, create the `base` class for actions, as can be seen in the following code:

```
using UnityEngine;
using System.Collections;

public class ActionBT : Task
{
    public override IEnumerator Run()
    {
        isFinished = false;
        // implement your behaviour here
        //---------
        return base.Run();
    }
}
```

7. Next, we're going to implement the `Selector` class, as shown in the following code:

```
using UnityEngine;
using System.Collections;

public class Selector : Task
{
    public override void SetResult(bool r)
    {
        if (r == true)
            isFinished = true;
    }

    public override IEnumerator RunTask()
    {
        foreach (Task t in children)
            yield return StartCoroutine(t.RunTask());
    }
}
```

8. Finally, we're also going to implement the `Sequence` class, which you can see in the following code:

```
using UnityEngine;
using System.Collections;

public class Sequence : Task
{
    public override void SetResult(bool r)
    {
        if (r == true)
```

```
                    isFinished = true;
        }

        public override IEnumerator RunTask()
        {
            foreach (Task t in children)
                yield return StartCoroutine(t.RunTask());
        }
    }
```

How it works...

Behavior trees work in a similar fashion to decision trees; however, the leaf nodes are called *tasks*, and there are some branch nodes that are not conditions, but run a set of tasks in one of two ways: `Selector` and `Sequence`. Selectors run a set of tasks and return true when one of their sub-tasks returns true. They can be seen as OR nodes. Sequences run a set of tasks and return true when all of their sub-tasks return true. They can be seen as AND nodes.

See also

- For more theoretical insights, refer to Ian Millington's book, *Artificial Intelligence for Games*.

Working with fuzzy logic

There are times when we have to deal with gray areas, instead of binary-based values, to make decisions, and **fuzzy logic** is a set of mathematical techniques that help us with this task.

Imagine that we're developing an automated driver. A couple of available actions are steering and speed control, both of which have a range of degrees. Deciding how to take a turn, and at what speed, is what will make our driver different and possibly smarter. That's the type of gray area that fuzzy logic helps represent and handle.

Getting ready

This recipe requires a set of states indexed by continuous integer numbers. As this representation varies from game to game, we handle the raw input from such states along with their *fuzzification* in order to have a good general-purpose, fuzzy decision maker. Finally, the decision maker returns a set of fuzzy values representing the degree of membership of each state.

How to do it...

In this section, we will be creating two base classes and our fuzzy decision maker:

1. First, we'll create the MembershipFunction parent class, as shown in the following screenshot:

```
using UnityEngine;
using System.Collections;

public class MembershipFunction : MonoBehaviour
{
    public int stateId;
    public virtual float GetDOM(object input)
    {
        return 0f;
    }
}
```

2. Next, we'll implement the FuzzyRule class, as follows:

```
using System.Collections;
using System.Collections.Generic;

public class FuzzyRule
{
    public List<int> stateIds;
    public int conclusionStateId;
}
```

3. Then we're going to create the `FuzzyDecisionMaker` class, as shown in the following code:

```
using UnityEngine;
using System.Collections;
using System.Collections.Generic;

public class FuzzyDecisionMaker : MonoBehaviour
{
}
```

4. We then define the decision-making function signature and its member variables, as demonstrated in the following code:

```
public Dictionary<int,float> MakeDecision(object[] inputs,
MembershipFunction[][] mfList, FuzzyRule[] rules)
{
    Dictionary<int, float> inputDOM = new Dictionary<int, float>();
    Dictionary<int, float> outputDOM = new Dictionary<int,
float>();
    MembershipFunction memberFunc;
    // next steps
}
```

5. Next, we're going to implement the loops for traversing the inputs, and populate the initial **degree of membership (DOM)** for each state. Take a look at the following code:

```
foreach (object input in inputs)
{
    int r, c;
    for (r = 0; r < mfList.Length; r++)
    {
        for (c = 0; c < mfList[r].Length; c++)
        {
            // next step
        }
    }
}
// steps after next
```

6. Then, we define the body of the innermost loop, which makes use of the proper membership functions to set (or update) the degrees of membership, as shown in the following code:

```
memberFunc = mfList[r][c];
int mfId = memberFunc.stateId;
```

```
float dom = memberFunc.GetDOM(input);
if (!inputDOM.ContainsKey(mfId))
{
    inputDOM.Add(mfId, dom);
    outputDOM.Add(mfId, 0f);
}
else
    inputDOM[mfId] = dom;
```

7. Then, we traverse the rules for setting the output degrees of membership, as shown in the following code:

```
foreach (FuzzyRule rule in rules)
{
    int outputId = rule.conclusionStateId;
    float best = outputDOM[outputId];
    float min = 1f;
    foreach (int state in rule.stateIds)
    {
        float dom = inputDOM[state];
        if (dom < best)
            continue;
        if (dom < min)
            min = dom;
    }
    outputDOM[outputId] = min;
}
```

8. Finally, we return the set of degrees of membership, as follows:

```
return outputDOM;
```

How it works...

We make use of the boxing/unboxing technique for handling any input via the object datatype. The *fuzzification* process is done with the help of our own membership functions, derived from the base class that we created in the beginning. Then, we take the minimum degree of membership for the input state for each rule, and calculate the final degree of membership for each output state given the maximum output from any of the applicable rules.

There's more...

We can create an example membership function to define whether an enemy is in enraged mode, knowing that its life points (ranging from zero to 100) are equal to or less than 30.

The following is the code for the example `MFEnraged` class:

```
using UnityEngine;
using System;
using System.Collections;

public class MFEnraged : MembershipFunction
{
    public override float GetDOM(object input)
    {
        if ((int)input <= 30)
            return 1f;
        return 0f;
    }
}
```

It's worth noting that it is a common requirement to have a complete set of rules; one for each combination of states from each input. This gives the recipe a lack of scalability, but it works well for a smaller number of input variables and a small number of states per variable.

See also

- For more theoretical insights regarding (de)*fuzzification* and scalability weaknesses, please refer to Ian Millington's book, *Artificial Intelligence for Games*.

Making decisions with goal-oriented behaviors

Goal-oriented behaviors are a set of techniques aimed to give agents not only a sense of intelligence, but also a sense of free will once a goal is defined and given a set of rules to choose from.

Imagine we're developing a trooper agent that need not only reach a goal of capturing the flag (main goal), but also while taking care of their own life and ammo (inner goals for reaching the first). One way of implementing it is to use a general-purpose algorithm for handling goals, so the agent develops something similar as free will.

Getting ready

We will learn how to create a goal-based action selector. Such a selector chooses an action, considering the main goal, avoiding unintentional actions with disrupting effects, and taking an action's duration into account. Just like the recipe in the preceding section, this requires the modeling of goals in terms of numerical values.

How to do it...

Along with the action chooser, we will create base classes for actions and goals:

1. First, we'll create the base class for modeling actions, as shown in the following code:

```csharp
using UnityEngine;
using System.Collections;

public class ActionGOB : MonoBehaviour
{
  public virtual float GetGoalChange(GoalGOB goal)
  {
    return 0f;
  }

  public virtual float GetDuration()
  {
    return 0f;
  }
}
```

2. Next, we'll create the GoalGOB parent class with member variables, as shown in the following code:

```csharp
using UnityEngine;
using System.Collections;

public class GoalGOB
{
```

```
   public string name;
   public float value;
   public float change;
}
```

3. Next, we'll define the proper functions for handling discontentment and change over time, as demonstrated in the following code:

```
public virtual float GetDiscontentment(float newValue)
{
  return newValue * newValue;
}

public virtual float GetChange()
{
  return 0f;
}
```

4. Then, we'll define the `ActionChooser` class, as shown in the following code:

```
using UnityEngine;
using System.Collections;

public class ActionChooser : MonoBehaviour
{
}
```

5. Next, we're implementing the function for handling unintentional actions, as shown in the following code:

```
public float CalculateDiscontentment(ActionGOB action, GoalGOB[]
goals)
{
  float discontentment = 0;
  foreach (GoalGOB goal in goals)
  {
    float newValue = goal.value + action.GetGoalChange(goal);
    newValue += action.GetDuration() * goal.GetChange();
    discontentment += goal.GetDiscontentment(newValue);
  }
  return discontentment;
}
```

6. Then, we implement the function for choosing an action, as follows:

```
public ActionGOB Choose(ActionGOB[] actions, GoalGOB[] goals)
{
  ActionGOB bestAction;
  bestAction = actions[0];
  float bestValue = CalculateDiscontentment(actions[0], goals);
  float value;
  // next steps
}
```

7. Next, we pick the best action based on the least compromising, as you can see in the following code:

```
foreach (ActionGOB action in actions)
{
  value = CalculateDiscontentment(action, goals);
  if (value < bestValue)
  {
    bestValue = value;
    bestAction = action;
  }
}
```

8. Finally, we return the best action, as shown in the following code:

```
return bestAction;
```

How it works...

The discontentment functions help avoid unintended actions, depending on how much a goal's value changes in terms of an action and the time it takes to be executed. Then, the function for choosing an action is handled by computing the best-promising in terms of the minimum impact (discontentment).

Implementing a blackboard architecture

In this recipe, we will model how we usually brainstorm and make decisions in an organized manner. First of all, this is called a **blackboard architecture**, or a **blackboard system**, based on the metaphor of a group of experts gathering in a room with a big blackboard. They're presented with a problem (facts, unknowns, and so on), and each is able to add/remove stuff from the board and give their opinion to solve the problem. The main issue is how to decide who takes the lead.

Let's say we have an RTS game to build a city, protect it, and conquer territories. For such a big task, it would be easier if we could implement modules for different problems as mentioned before: build and sustain, protect, and attack. In that regard, we need submodules (experts) that allow us to compartmentalize knowledge and decisions. Depending on the current state of the game, one expert is given control to take actions that will allow us to reach the current goal.

In the following sections, we will elaborate on a solution to such an issue.

Getting ready

We need to define certain data structures for setting up everything before implementing the main steps:

1. First, we'll create the data structure for handling data bits in a flexible manner, as shown in the following code:

```
public struct BlackboardDatum
{
  public int id;
  public string type;
  public object value;
}
```

2. Next, we'll create the class defining the expert, as follows:

```
public abstract class BlackboardExpert
{
  public virtual float GetInsistence(Blackboard board)
  {
    return 0f;
  }
  public virtual void Run(Blackboard board){}
}
```

3. Then, we create the data structure for saving actions taken by the experts, as shown in the following code:

```
public struct BlackboardAction
{
  public object expert;
  public string name;
  public System.Action action;
}
```

How to do it...

Now, let's create the class that handles the blackboard and the main logic behind our metaphor:

1. First, let's define the `Blackboard` class, as shown in the following code:

```
using System.Collections.Generic;

public class Blackboard
{
  public List<BlackboardDatum> entries;
  public List<BlackboardAction> pastActions;
  public List<BlackboardExpert> experts;
}
```

2. Next, let's implement its constructor, as follows:

```
public Blackboard()
{
  entries = new List<BlackboardDatum>();
  pastActions = new List<BlackboardAction>();
  experts = new List<BlackboardExpert>();
}
```

3. Then, we can define the main class for each iteration, as shown in the following code:

```
public void RunIteration()
{
  // next steps
}
```

4. Next, we're going to add the required variables, as you'll see in the following code:

```
BlackboardExpert bestExpert = null;
float maxInsistence = 0f;
```

5. Then, we'll implement the loop for deciding which expert will run next, as demonstrated in the following code:

```
foreach (BlackboardExpert e in experts)
{
  float insistence = e.GetInsistence(this);
  if (insistence > maxInsistence)
  {
```

```
            maxInsistence = insistence;
            bestExpert = e;
        }
    }
```

6. Now, if there's an expert chosen, make it run, as shown in the following code:

```
if (bestExpert != null)
  bestExpert.Run(this);
```

How it works...

First, we put in place all the data structures for creating the blackboard system to be unopinionated, and flexible enough for reuse. Then, we put in place the blackboard, and the main loop for deciding which expert will run next. It's pretty similar to the behavior-blending algorithm by priority, developed in `Chapter 1`, *Behaviors – Intelligent Movement*, but it's applied to solving a problem. Each expert computes how much it *thinks* that their opinion is important, and the most relevant one takes its turn to solve the problem. It's important to define the range of values returning from the `GetInsistence` function.

There's more...

We need to implement our own member functions by overriding the member functions from the `Expert` class. It's important to note that it's up to each expert to read and write the blackboard entries in the `GetInsistence` function. Then, it's time to execute actions during the `Run` member function. If the experts' `Run` member functions are computationally expensive, it's better to handle them via coroutines.

Finally, this could be revisited on each project by defining the blackboard as the game state, on which each expert is able to read and write data. Just keep in mind the priority part of the algorithm for it to run as expected.

Experimenting with Unity's animation state machine

We usually see a lot of things going on in Unity's animation state machine graph when we work alongside artists focused on animations, or when we use our own if we have a thing for this discipline; however, it's uncommon seeing things happening in code on top of it. We usually change states via the MonoBehaviour script, and deal with the behaviors in a separate manner.

In this recipe, we will use some of the basic movement behaviors created in Chapter 1, *Behaviors – Intelligent Movement*, as they are, and we will make our animator control their status.

Getting ready

This recipe doesn't cover the setting up of the animations in the **Animator** window. It's up to the reader to set them up. We will focus on the required steps for leveraging the power of the built-in finite-state machine to control our agent.

How to do it...

Let's set everything up first:

1. First, create a new **Animator Controller** using the **Create** button in the **Project** window, as shown in the following screenshot:

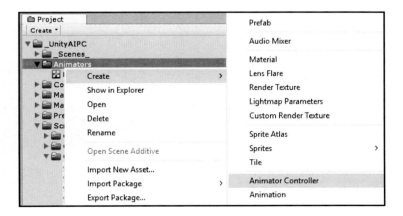

2. Next, create a new default state called **Wandering**.
3. Then, create a new state called **Pursuing**.
4. Next, connect both states to each other, and back, with two transitions, as you'll see in the following screenshot:

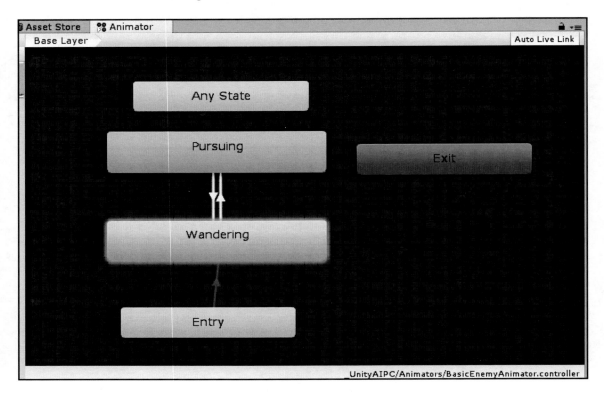

5. Now, we create two trigger parameters: `Pursue` and `Wander`, as shown in the following screenshot:

6. Next, assign the `Wander` parameter to the set of conditions in the **Pursuing -> Wandering** transition, as demonstrated in the following screenshot:

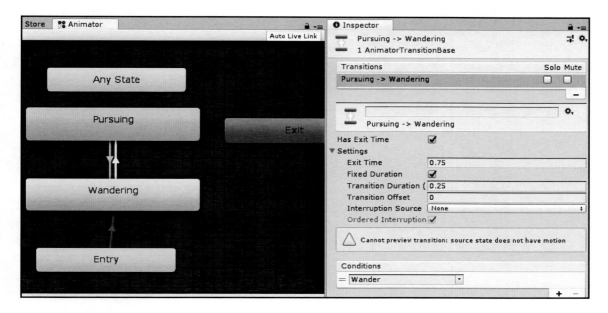

7. Next, make the inverse assignment in the **Wandering -> Pursuing** transition.

8. Then, we need to create a script behavior on the `Wander` state called `AFSMWandering`, as you can see in the following screenshot:

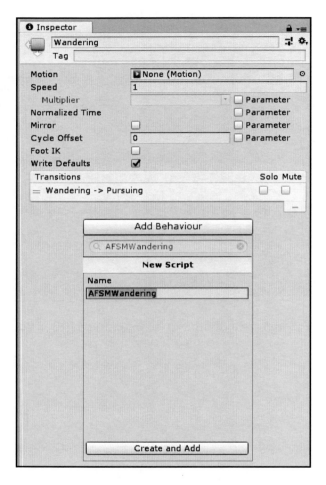

9. We then create a script behavior on the `Pursue` state called `AFSMPursue`, using the preceding method.
10. Next, create a new **GameObject** called `Wanderer`, and attach the following components:
    - **Animator**
    - **Agent**
    - **Wander** (disabled)
    - **Seek** (disabled)

The following image shows what the game object should look like. See how it shows the components mentioned in the preceeding step:

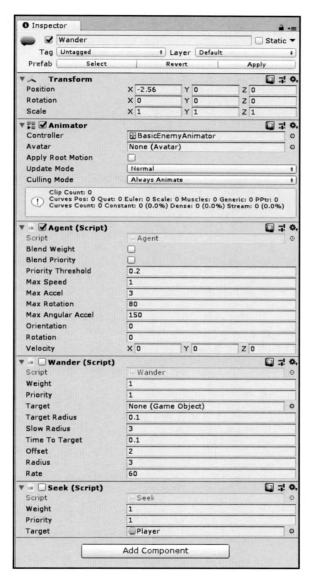

Animator, Agent, Wander, and Seek components attached to a game object

Now, we will implement the `Wander` state:

1. First, let's open the `AFSMWanderer.cs` file created previously.
2. Then, add the following member variables shown in the following code:

```
public float pursueDistance = 3f;
private Wander _wander;
private Seek _pursue;
```

3. Next, uncomment the `OnStateEnter` member function.
4. Then, we add code to it, as demonstrated in the following code:

```
AgentBehavior[] behaviors;
GameObject gameObject = animator.gameObject;
behaviors = gameObject.GetComponents<AgentBehavior>();
foreach (AgentBehavior b in behaviors)
  b.enabled = false;

_wander = gameObject.GetComponent<Wander>();
_pursue = gameObject.GetComponent<Seek>();
if (_wander == null || _pursue == null)
  return;
_wander.enabled = true;
animator.gameObject.name = "Wandering";
```

5. Uncomment the `OnStateUpdate` member function.
6. Then add code to it, as follows:

```
Vector3 targetPos, agentPos;
targetPos = _pursue.target.transform.position;
agentPos = animator.transform.position;
float distance = Vector3.Distance(targetPos, agentPos);
if (distance > pursueDistance)
    return;
animator.SetTrigger("Pursue");
```

Finally, we will implement a similar code in our `Pursue` state:

1. First, let's open the `AFSMPursue.cs` file created previously.
2. Next, add the member variables as shown in the following code:

```
public float stopDistance = 8f;
private Wander _wander;
private Seek _pursue;
```

3. Uncomment the `OnStateEnter` member function.

4. Next, add code as follows:

```
AgentBehavior[] behaviors;
GameObject gameObject = animator.gameObject;
behaviors = gameObject.GetComponents<AgentBehavior>();
foreach (AgentBehavior b in behaviors)
  b.enabled = false;

_wander = gameObject.GetComponent<Wander>();
_pursue = gameObject.GetComponent<Seek>();
if (_wander == null || _pursue == null)
  return;
_pursue.enabled = true;
animator.gameObject.name = "Seeking";
```

5. Uncomment the `OnStateUpdate` member function.

6. Finally, add the following code to it:

```
Vector3 targetPos, agentPos;
targetPos = _pursue.target.transform.position;
agentPos = animator.transform.position;
if (Vector3.Distance(targetPos, agentPos) < stopDistance)
  return;
animator.SetTrigger("Wander");
```

How it works...

We have the finite-state machine system that is the animator engine. First, we create the states and transitions that the agent will have. Second, we create our own behaviors deriving from the `StateMachineBehaviour` class, and attach them to the corresponding state. Also, we retrieve information needed from our game objects and script components to make decisions inside of each state. If required, we call the proper trigger to change states, thus changing the agent's behavior.

There's more...

By working on top of Unity's animation state machine, we gain a lot of flexibility. This way, we can reuse behaviors and decision making among several agents with minimum code and setup; however, what we gain in flexibility and modularity, we lose in script centralization. It is important to take that into account when working in teams, and even to remember that for debugging purposes (it happened while writing this book, LOL).

The New NavMesh API

4

In this chapter, we will learn how to make use of the new NavMesh API, through the following recipes:

- Setting up the NavMesh building components
- Creating and managing NavMesh for multiple types of agents
- Creating and updating NavMesh data at runtime
- Controlling the lifetime of the NavMesh instance
- Connecting multiple instances of NavMesh
- Creating dynamic NavMeshes with obstacles
- Implementing some behaviors using the NavMesh API

Introduction

The introduction of the NavMesh API, and its expansion, has opened a whole new world for AI and gameplay developers. It allows us to better tune our levels, even in real time, without the use of external tools (at least for a wide range of options).

In this chapter, we will learn how to manipulate this new set of tools that run on top of an already known and powerful navigation engine.

Setting up the NavMesh building components

Before manipulating our level and getting the hang of all the recipes, we need to download some assets from Unity's GitHub repository.

Getting ready

Some of us probably have some experience with the navigation engine that Unity has included for quite some time. It is important to have grasped the basics of creating a NavMesh by baking them via the **Navigation** window, and to understand the basics of the NavMeshAgent component.

How to do it...

To download the assets from the GitHub repository:

1. Go to the following web address using your preferred browser: `https://github.com/Unity-Technologies/NavMeshComponents`.

2. Go to the **releases** section, located under the **Code** tab as shown:

3. Download the compressed file to your computer, according to your version of Unity. In our case, it's `2018.1.0f2` at the time of writing.

4. Decompress the file outside the main project. We can see that it is a Unity project on its own:

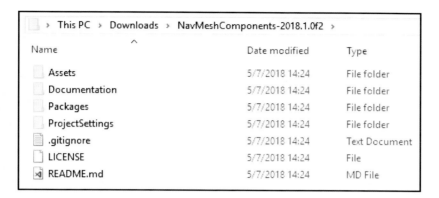

5. Navigate to the `Assets` folder, where we will see the following:

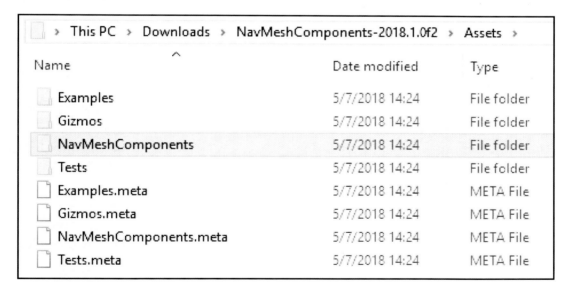

6. Copy or move the `NavMeshComponents` folder, with all its content, into your target project's `Asset` folder:

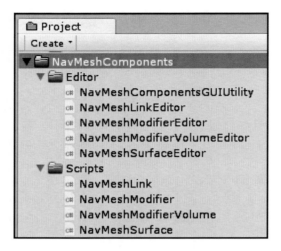

7. Let Unity reload the assets.

How it works...

By including this set of scripts, we have moved one step forward into automating the creation of navigation meshes as we please, even in real time. We could use the low-level API to create more complex components by taking a look at the scripts that are included in the zipped folder we just added to our project.

There's more...

One way to test that we carried out the previous steps successfully is to take the following steps:

1. Check there are no errors after asset reloading.
2. Create an empty game object, or select a random one for testing.
3. Go to the **Inspector** window and click on **Add Component**.
4. Write `NavMesh` in the search bar.

5. Make sure that all of the following components are listed:
    - **Nav Mesh Agent** (included in Unity)
    - **Nav Mesh Obstacle** (included in Unity)
    - **NavMeshLink**
    - **NavMeshModifier**
    - **NavMeshModifierVolume**
    - **NavMeshSurface**

See also

For further information and references on the whole Navigation system, and the NavMesh building components, please refer to the official documentation available at these links:

- `https://docs.unity3d.com/Manual/Navigation.html`
- `https://docs.unity3d.com/Manual/NavMesh-BuildingComponents.html`

Creating and managing NavMesh for multiple types of agents

Our levels can have different areas that may change the behavior of our agents; say lava, a swamp, doors, and so on. In that case, we will need some kind of representation so that the agents are unable to pass those areas, change their speed, or simply devise a better route to avoid hazardous zones.

In this recipe, we will learn how to implement those areas in our level, so we have a more complex navigation mesh for our agents to handle better behavior.

Getting ready

Swamps, shallow water, and lava are easily placed in a level, and tagged on as a navigation area. However, doors are a little different. In this case, we will need to place an object below our door arc. It's even better if the door/arc mesh has a base mesh already. The following screenshot shows an example of what we're talking about:

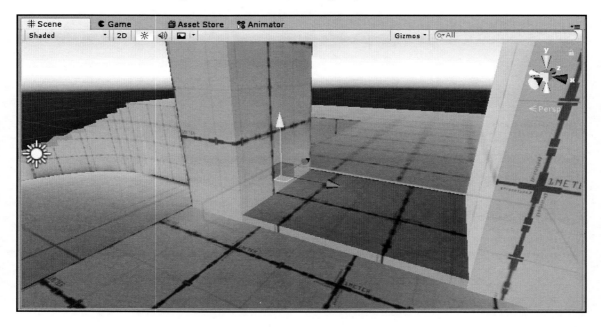

Door object below visual door for players

How to do it...

Now, we will learn how to make the proper changes to the NavMesh settings before baking:

1. Create the game world with different areas. In our case, we will have regular areas (walkable), doors, and swamps.
2. Open the **Navigation** window: **Menu | Window | Navigation**.
3. Go to the **Areas** tab.
4. Create a `Swamp` area with cost 6.
5. Create a `Door` area with cost 2.

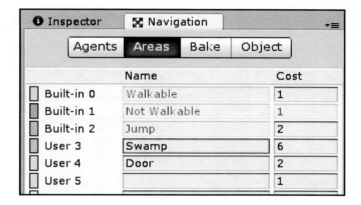

6. Select the objects that will behave like swamps.
7. Go to the **Navigation** window, and select the **Objects** tab.
8. Change the **Navigation Area** value to **Swamp**.
9. Select the objects that will behave like doors.
10. Go to the **Navigation** window, and select the **Objects** tab.
11. Change the **Navigation Area** value to **Door**.

12. Bake the NavMesh:

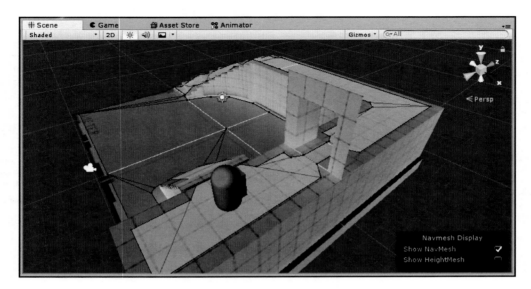

Resulting baked NavMesh

Then, we need to set up the agents so they behave as intended with the designated areas:

1. Add the agent object to the scene.
2. Add the **NavMesh** component to the object.
3. Go to the **Inspector** window.
4. Select the available areas that the agent can traverse. In our case, deselect the **Door** area mask:

NavMeshAgent configuration for enemies that cannot walk through doors

How it works...

As seen in the preceding section, the navigation mesh is divided into different areas thanks to our settings. When implementing the search algorithm for devising a path to the target location, the agent takes into account the weights we defined for each area. As stated in the documentation, Unity implements A*, so the agent takes the cheapest path. It also takes into account only the areas we selected. That's why we deselected the doors, so players can hide behind them and find refuge.

There's more...

We could also make use of the current area, so the agent behaves differently (changes speed, for example). In that case, we need to get to know the `SamplePathPostion` from the **NavMeshAgent** component.

Creating and updating NavMesh data at runtime

With the advent of procedural-generated content, more specifically levels, it becomes necessary to come up with techniques that enable us to adjust the navigation areas. This is also important when we have very dynamic levels that can be destroyed in real time in a non-scripted way.

Getting ready

It is important to have the `NavMeshComponents` directory in our project as shown in the previous recipe, *Setting up our project*.

Also, it is important to attach the **NavMeshSurface** component to all the parent objects we want to build the new navigation mesh with.

How to do it...

We will create a new component called **NavMeshBuilder**:

1. Create a new file called `NavMeshBuilder.cs`:

```
using UnityEngine;
using UnityEngine.AI;
using System.Collections;
using System.Collections.Generic;

public class NavMeshBuilder : MonoBehaviour
{
   // Next steps
}
```

2. Add a member variable for storing the navigation surfaces:

```
public NavMeshSurface[] surfaces;
```

3. Implement the method for building all the `NavMesh` at once:

```
public void Build()
{
   for (int i = 0; i < surfaces.Length; i++)
   {
      surfaces[i].BuildNavMesh();
   }
}
```

4. Implement the method for building all the `NavMesh` in between frames:

```
public IEnumerator BuildInFrames(System.Action eventHandler)
{
   for (int i = 0; i < surfaces.Length; i++)
   {
      surfaces[i].BuildNavMesh();
      yield return null;
   }
   if (eventHandler != null)
      eventHandler.Invoke();
}
```

How it works...

By importing the `NavMeshComponents` directory, we are able to manipulate meshes and their surfaces via the **NavMeshSurface** component, using their *up* vector to detect the movement areas.

In the second member function, we take advantage of the coroutines' system to avoid freezing our game in case a surface is too complex to handle fast. Also, we make use of the delegate system to trigger an event when all the navigation meshes have been built on all the surfaces.

Controlling the lifetime of the NavMesh instance

Occasionally, we need to create navigation on the go because the topology is unknown. This is crucial when dealing with procedural-generated levels. One of the options is to bake the NavMesh at runtime, as we learned before. However, it could be a problem if level topology is really big or complex. Luckily, the **NavMesh** components developed by Unity can help us with this task, taking a different approach.

In this recipe, we will learn how to create a NavMesh around an agent without a NavMesh volume, making use of the NavMesh components.

Getting started

It is important to have the `NavMeshComponents` directory in our project, as shown in the previous recipe, *Setting up our project*.

How to do it...

1. Create the game level with proper colliders on the floor and/or the terrain where the agent will navigate.
2. Create the agent object with the following components set up: **Capsule** or **Box Collider**, **Rigidbody**, and **NavMesh Agent**.

3. Create the `NMRealTimeBuilder` class:

```
using UnityEngine;
using UnityEngine.AI;
using System.Collections;
using System.Collections.Generic;
using NavMeshBuilder = UnityEngine.AI.NavMeshBuilder;

public class NMRealTimeBuilder : MonoBehaviour
{
  // next steps
}
```

4. Declare the required member variables:

```
public Transform agent;
public Vector3 boxSize = new Vector3(50f, 20f, 50f);
[Range(0.01f, 1f)]
public float sizeChange = 0.1f;
private NavMeshData navMesh;
private AsyncOperation operation;
private NavMeshDataInstance navMeshInstance;
private List<NavMeshBuildSource> sources = new
List<NavMeshBuildSource>();
```

5. Implement the `static` member function for comparing the difference between two cubes:

```
static private Vector3 Quantize(Vector3 a, Vector3 q)
{
  float x = q.x * Mathf.Floor(a.x/q.x);
  float y = q.y * Mathf.Floor(a.y/q.y);
  float z = q.z * Mathf.Floor(a.z/q.z);
  return new Vector3(x, y, z);
}
```

6. Implement the member function that makes use of the previous function:

```
private Bounds QuantizeBounds()
{
  Vector3 position = agent.transform.position;
  return new Bounds(Quantize(position, boxSize * sizeChange),
boxSize);
}
```

7. Define the member function for updating the NavMesh around the agent:

```
private void UpdateNavMesh(bool isAsync = false)
{
  // next step
}
```

8. Implement the member function declared before:

```
NavMeshSourceTag.Collect(ref sources);
NavMeshBuildSettings settings;
settings = NavMesh.GetSettingsByID(0);
Bounds bounds = QuantizeBounds();
if (isAsync)
  operation = NavMeshBuilder.UpdateNavMeshDataAsync(navMesh,
settings, sources, bounds);
else
 NavMeshBuilder.UpdateNavMeshData(navMesh, settings, sources,
bounds);
```

9. Implement the Awake member function:

```
private void Awake()
{
  if (agent == null)
    agent = transform;
}
```

10. Implement the OnEnable member function:

```
private void OnEnable()
{
  navMesh = new NavMeshData();
  navMeshInstance = NavMesh.AddNavMeshData(navMesh);
  UpdateNavMesh(false);
}
```

11. Implement the OnDisable member function:

```
private void OnDisable()
{
  navMeshInstance.Remove();
}
```

How it works...

We leverage the power of the **NavMesh** components to create a smaller component that helps us in building a custom NavMesh around the object.

We take the size of the box around our agent, and the required difference between the box around the previous frame and the current one. If that difference is greater than the percentage we declared in `sizeChange`, the `NavMeshBuilder` takes the new position, disposes of the previous navigation mesh, and creates a new one.

That way, we can have an unknown topology, but can navigate it with the same type of agent. Furthermore, it takes considerably less time because we're using the size variable (a `Vector3`) to create the bounds.

There's more...

The `NMRealTimeBuilder` component could be attached to the very agent game object or to a different one. That's why we implemented the `Awake` function.

Finally, we could use a mix between the recipe and some of the behaviors developed in `Chapter 1`, *Behaviors – Intelligent Movement*, by getting the direction of the target and then telling the agent to walk to the farthest point of the NavMesh in that direction.

Connecting multiple instances of NavMesh

We have learned how to build a NavMesh, but there are cases where levels are really complex to the point of needing to divide them in several sections; sometimes, this is because there are pitfalls or because we are loading our level programmatically.

Getting ready

It is important to work on top of objects that have at least one **NavMeshSurface** component attached.

How to do it...

We need to connect one **NavMeshSurface** component to another one:

1. Locate, via the editor or code, two **NavMeshSurface** components to connect
2. Add the **NavMeshLink** component to the object that will work as the origin
3. Select the agent type that will be able to use the connection
4. Set the **Start Point** and **End Point** values
5. Repeat the previous steps for every agent type for which you need to connect the nodes

How it works...

Imagine one **NavMeshSurface** component working as a big node in a graph. By using the **NavMeshLink** component, we add an edge between two nodes. It's worth noting that the coordinates in **Start Point** and **End Point** are relative to the object; thus, they move/rotate with the parent object.

There's more...

We might need some special actions between transitions, such as animations. Imagine a one-directional link between a ledge and the ground. We have the power to know exactly when the agent hits the link, and then we can play an animation.

One way to do this is by deactivating the **Auto Traverse Off-Mesh Links** option on the **NavMeshAgent** component, playing the animation, executing the physics, and continuing with the logic as planned.

Creating dynamic NavMeshes with obstacles

There are times when our levels have dynamic obstacles and we need the agent to avoid those obstacles as well. Let's imagine an MMORPG or a MOBA, where the minions from our hero also need to avoid obstacles in order to reach the target. We could implement a difficult algorithm to blend the navigation with the obstacle avoidance, or we could leverage the power of a dynamic NavMesh to get the same result, with little to no code disruption.

In this recipe, we will learn how to adapt a NavMesh to be dynamic and react to moving obstacles, so our agents can avoid them and reach the target successfully.

Getting ready

It is important to know how the NavMesh basics work, and how to build/bake a NavMesh.

How to do it...

1. Put the level in place.
2. Create an empty game object and call it `NavMesh`.
3. Add the **NavMeshSurface** component to the **NavMesh** object.
4. Hit **Bake**.
5. Select all the obstacles.
6. Add the **Nav Mesh Obstacle** component to them.
7. Check the **Carve** option in the component.
8. Select the dynamic obstacles.
9. Uncheck the **Carve Only Stationary** option.
10. Configure each obstacle as needed, using the other options in the component.

How it works...

After baking the initial navigation mesh, the whole system takes into account all the obstacles in the scene and carves the areas around the obstacles in order to fine-tune the available navigation area. Besides, the navigation system keeps track of the dynamic obstacles' transformations (the ones with the **Carve Only Stationary** option unchecked) in order to recalculate the navigation area as needed.

There's more...

The aforementioned process is definitely not performance friendly, and works best in cases where we don't know for sure the topology, such as in procedural-generated levels. Although we put in place the example with a known level, we can rely on prefabs and programming to recreate most of the previous steps and apply them in a procedural-generated level.

On the other hand, if we know for sure the level's layout and want to improve performance, we could leave the **Carve** option unchecked in the **Nav Mesh Obstacle** component, and play with the obstacle avoidance parameters (found in the **Nav Mesh Agent** component) until we get a result that satisfies our needs.

Finally, we could just play around with a mixed method to find a balance between performance and experience, selecting key obstacles to be avoided with our "good enough" parameters and other obstacles that affect the navigation mesh in real time.

See also

For more details on dynamic navigation meshes, please refer to the official Unity video found at `https://unity3d.com/learn/tutorials/topics/navigation/making-it-dynamic`.

Implementing some behaviors using the NavMesh API

In `Chapter 1`, *Behaviors – Intelligent Movement*, we learned about different types of movement for our agents. We can implement some of them in a different way using the NavMesh API and the **NavMeshAgent** component. Thus, we'll be able to prototype similar behaviors in a faster, cleaner, and more Unity-ish way.

We will learn how to implement the patrolling behavior so that we can have a different angle and get ideas on how to fast-prototype different behaviors beyond the basic flow.

Getting ready

It is important to have grasped the basics of NavMesh and baking and handling the **NavMeshAgent** component before working on this recipe.

How to do it...

We will create a patrol behavior component to be used along with a **NavMeshAgent** component:

1. Create a script named `NMPatrol.cs`, and include the `NavMeshAgent` as a required component:

```
using UnityEngine;
using UnityEngine.AI;

[RequireComponent(typeof(NavMeshAgent))]
public class NMPatrol : MonoBehaviour
{
    // next steps
}
```

2. Add the member variables required:

```
public float pointDistance = 0.5f;
public Transform[] patrolPoints;
private int currentPoint = 0;
private NavMeshAgent agent;
```

3. Create a function for finding the closest patrol point in the array:

```
private int FindClosestPoint()
{
    // next step
}
```

4. Add the internal variables required:

```
int index = -1;
float distance = Mathf.Infinity;
int i;
Vector3 agentPosition = transform.position;
Vector3 pointPosition;
```

5. Implement the loop for finding the closest point:

```
for (i = 0; i < patrolPoints.Length; i++)
{
    pointPosition = patrolPoints[i].position;
    float d = Vector3.Distance(agentPosition, pointPosition);
    if (d < distance)
    {
        index = i;
```

```
        distance = d;
    }
  }
  return index;
```

6. Implement the function for updating the agent's destination point:

```
private void GoToPoint(int next)
{
  if (next < 0 || next >= patrolPoints.Length)
    return;
  agent.destination = patrolPoints[next].position;
}
```

7. Implement the `Start` function for initialization:

```
private void Start()
{
  agent = GetComponent<NavMeshAgent>();
  agent.autoBraking = false;
  currentPoint = FindClosestPoint();
  GoToPoint(currentPoint);
}
```

8. Implement the `Update` function:

```
private void Update()
{
  if (!agent.pathPending && agent.remainingDistance <
pointDistance)
    GoToPoint((currentPoint + 1) % patrolPoints.Length);
}
```

How it works...

We have a patrolling component that requires the navigation agent controller to work as intended. First, we calculate the closest point to the agent and move it to that position. After that, we use the `pointDistance` value to make the agent aware that it needs to move to the next point in the loop. Finally, we use the modulo operation to get the next patrol point without too much validation and just keep increasing the number of the current point.

There's more...

We need to take into account the order in which we put the patrol points in the array, so that they work as intended. Also, we could work on this a little bit by creating a function for deciding what the next patrol point will be. This will come in handy if we decide to keep improving the patrolling behavior according to our game's requirements:

```
private int CalculateNextPoint()
{
  return (currentPoint + 1) % patrolPoints.Length;
}

private void Update()
{
  if (!agent.pathPending && agent.remainingDistance < pointDistance)
    GoToPoint(CalculateNextPoint());
}
```

5
Coordination and Tactics

In this chapter, we will learn techniques for coordination and devising tactics:

- Handling formations
- Extending A* for coordination: A*mbush
- Introducing waypoints by making a manual selector
- Analyzing waypoints by height
- Analyzing waypoints by cover and visibility
- Creating waypoints automatically
- Exemplifying waypoints for decision making
- Implementing influence maps
- Improving influence with map flooding
- Improving influence with convolution filters
- Building a fighting circle

Introduction

As we will see, this is not a chapter focused on a sole subject, but rather a chapter that has its own original recipes and also draws on previous recipes in order to create new or improved techniques.

In this chapter, we will learn different recipes for coordinating different agents as a whole organism, such as formations and techniques that allow us to make tactical decisions based on graphs (such as waypoints) and influence maps. These techniques use different elements from the previous chapters and recipes, especially from graph construction and path-finding algorithms found in `Chapter 2`, *Navigation*.

Handling formations

This is a key algorithm for creating flocks or a group of military agents. It is designed to be flexible enough to give you the chance to create your own formations.

The end result of this recipe is having a set of target positions and rotations for each agent in the formation. Then, it is up to you to create the necessary algorithms to move the agent to the previous targets.

 We can use the movement algorithms learned in `Chapter 1`, *Behaviors – Intelligent Movement*, in order to target these positions.

Getting ready

We will need to create three base classes that are the data types to be used by the high-level classes and algorithms. The `Location` class is very similar to the `Steering` class and is used to define a target position and rotation given the formation's anchor point and rotation. The `SlogAssignment` class is a data type to match a list's indices and agents. Finally, the `Character` class is a component to hold the target `Location` class.

The following is the code for the `Location` class:

```
using UnityEngine;
using System.Collections;

public class Location
{
    public Vector3 position;
    public Quaternion rotation;

    public Location ()
    {
        position = Vector3.zero;
        rotation = Quaternion.identity;
```

```
        }

        public Location(Vector3 position, Quaternion rotation)
        {
            this.position = position;
            this.rotation = rotation;
        }
    }
```

The following is the code for the SlotAssignment class:

```
using UnityEngine;
using System.Collections;

public class SlotAssignment
{
    public int slotIndex;
    public GameObject character;

    public SlotAssignment()
    {
        slotIndex = -1;
        character = null;
    }
}
```

The following is the code for the Character class:

```
using UnityEngine;
using System.Collections;

public class Character : MonoBehaviour
{
    public Location location;

    public void SetTarget (Location location)
    {
        this.location = location;
    }
}
```

How to do it...

We will implement two classes—`FormationPattern` and `FormationManager`:

1. Create the `FormationPattern` pseudo-abstract class:

```
using UnityEngine;
using System.Collections;
using System.Collections.Generic;

public class FormationPattern: MonoBehaviour
{
    public int numOfSlots;
    public GameObject leader;
}
```

2. Implement the `Start` function:

```
void Start()
{
    if (leader == null)
        leader = transform.gameObject;
}
```

3. Define the function for getting the position for a given slot:

```
public virtual Vector3 GetSlotLocation(int slotIndex)
{
    return Vector3.zero;
}
```

4. Define the function for retrieving, if a given number of slots is supported by the formation:

```
public bool SupportsSlots(int slotCount)
{
    return slotCount <= numOfSlots;
}
```

5. Implement the function for setting an offset in the locations, if necessary:

```
public virtual Location GetDriftOffset(List<SlotAssignment>
slotAssignments)
{
    Location location = new Location();
    location.position = leader.transform.position;
    location.rotation = leader.transform.rotation;
    return location;
}
```

6. Create the class for managing the formation:

```
using UnityEngine;
using System.Collections;
using System.Collections.Generic;

public class FormationManager : MonoBehaviour
{
    public FormationPattern pattern;
    private List<SlotAssignment> slotAssignments;
    private Location driftOffset;
}
```

7. Implement the Awake function:

```
void Awake()
{
    slotAssignments = new List<SlotAssignment>();
}
```

8. Define the function for updating the slot assignments given the list's order:

```
public void UpdateSlotAssignments()
{
    for (int i = 0; i < slotAssignments.Count; i++)
    {
        slotAssignments[i].slotIndex = i;
    }
    driftOffset = pattern.GetDriftOffset(slotAssignments);
}
```

9. Implement the function for adding a character to the formation:

```
public bool AddCharacter(GameObject character)
{
    int occupiedSlots = slotAssignments.Count;
    if (!pattern.SupportsSlots(occupiedSlots + 1))
        return false;
    SlotAssignment sa = new SlotAssignment();
    sa.character = character;
    slotAssignments.Add(sa);
    UpdateSlotAssignments();
    return true;
}
```

10. Implement the function for removing a character in the formation:

```
public void RemoveCharacter(GameObject agent)
{
    int index = slotAssignments.FindIndex(x =>
x.character.Equals(agent));
    slotAssignments.RemoveAt(index);
    UpdateSlotAssignments();
}
```

11. Implement the function for updating the slots:

```
public void UpdateSlots()
{
    GameObject leader = pattern.leader;
    Vector3 anchor = leader.transform.position;
    Vector3 slotPos;
    Quaternion rotation;
    rotation = leader.transform.rotation;
    foreach (SlotAssignment sa in slotAssignments)
    {
        // next step
    }
}
```

12. Finally, implement the `foreach` loop:

```
Vector3 relPos;
slotPos = pattern.GetSlotLocation(sa.slotIndex);
relPos = anchor;
relPos += leader.transform.TransformDirection(slotPos);
Location charDrift = new Location(relPos, rotation);
Character character = sa.character.GetComponent<Character>();
character.SetTarget(charDrift);
```

How it works...

The `FormationPattern` class contains the relative positions for a given slot. For example, a `CircleFormation` child class will implement the `GetSlotLocation` class, given the number of slots and its locations over 360 degrees. It is intended to be a basic class, so it is up to the manager to add a layer for permissions and rearrangement. That way, the designer can focus on simple formation scripting, deriving from the base class.

The `FormationManager` class, as stated earlier, handles the high-level layer and arranges the locations as it better fits the formation's needs and permissions. The calculations are based on top of the leader's position and rotation, and they apply the necessary transformations given the pattern's principles.

There's more...

It is worth mentioning that the `FormationManager` and `FormationPattern` classes are intended to be components of the same object. When the leader field in the manager is set to `null`, the leader is the object itself. This way, we could have a different leader object in order to have a clean inspector window and class modularity.

See also

For further information on the theory behind this recipe, you can refer to the following materials:

- `Chapter 1`, *Behaviors – Intelligent Movement*, in the recipe, *Arriving and Leaving*.
- Ian Millington's book, *Artificial Intelligence for Games*.

Extending A* for coordination – A*mbush

After learning how to implement A* for path finding, we will now use its power and flexibility to develop some kind of coordinated behavior in order to ambush the player. This algorithm is especially useful when we want an inexpensive solution for the aforementioned problem, and which also has ease of implementation.

This recipe sets the path for every agent, to be taken into account for ambushing a given vertex or point in the graph.

Getting ready

We need a special component for the agents called `Lurker`. This class will hold the paths that are to be used later in the navigation process.

The following is the code for the `Lurker` class:

```
using UnityEngine;
using System.Collections;
using System.Collections.Generic;

public class Lurker : MonoBehaviour
{
    [HideInInspector]
    public List<int> pathIds;
    [HideInInspector]
    public List<GameObject> pathObjs;

    void Awake()
    {
        if (pathIds == null)
            pathIds = new List<int>();
        if (pathObjs == null)
            pathObjs = new List<GameObject>();
    }
}
```

How to do it...

We will create the main function for setting the ambush path for all the agents and then the function for setting each agent's path:

1. Define the main function for the ambush:

    ```
    public void SetPathAmbush(GameObject dstObj, List<Lurker> lurkers)
    {
        Vertex dst = GetNearestVertex(dstObj.transform.position);
        foreach (Lurker l in lurkers)
        {
            Vertex src = GetNearestVertex(l.transform.position);
            l.path = AStarMbush(src, dst, l, lurkers);
        }
    }
    ```

2. Declare the function for finding each path:

```
public List<Vertex> AStarMbush(
        Vertex src,
        Vertex dst,
        Lurker agent,
        List<Lurker> lurkers,
        Heuristic h = null)
{     // next steps
}
```

3. Declare the necessary members for handling the extra cost of computations:

```
int graphSize = vertices.Count;
float[] extra = new float[graphSize];
float[] costs = new float[graphSize];
int i;
```

4. Initialize the regular cost and the extra cost variables:

```
for (i = 0; i < graphSize; i++)
{
    extra[i] = 1f;
    costs[i] = Mathf.Infinity;
}
```

5. Add the extra cost to each vertex that is contained in another agent's path:

```
foreach (Lurker l in lurkers)
{
    foreach (Vertex v in l.path)
    {
        extra[v.id] += 1f;
    }
}
```

6. Declare and initialize the variables for computing A*:

```
Edge[] successors;
int[] previous = new int[graphSize];
for (i = 0; i < graphSize; i++)
    previous[i] = -1;
previous[src.id] = src.id;
float cost = 0;
Edge node = new Edge(src, 0);
GPWiki.BinaryHeap<Edge> frontier = new GPWiki.BinaryHeap<Edge>();
```

7. Start implementing the A* main loop:

```
frontier.Add(node);
while (frontier.Count != 0)
{
    if (frontier.Count == 0)
        return new List<GameObject>();
    // next steps
}
return new List<Vertex>();
```

8. Validate that the goal has already been reached, otherwise it's not worth computing the costs, and you'd be better off continuing with the usual A* algorithm:

```
node = frontier.Remove();
if (ReferenceEquals(node.vertex, dst))
    return BuildPath(src.id, node.vertex.id, ref previous);
int nodeId = node.vertex.id;
if (node.cost > costs[nodeId])
    continue;
```

9. Traverse the neighbors and check whether they have been visited:

```
successors = GetEdges(node.vertex);
foreach (Edge e in successors)
{
    int eId = e.vertex.id;
    if (previous[eId] != -1)
        continue;
    // next step
}
```

10. If they haven't been visited, add them to the `frontier`:

```
cost = e.cost;
cost += costs[dst.id];
cost += h(e.vertex, dst);
if (cost < costs[e.vertex.id])
{
    Edge child;
    child = new Edge(e.vertex, cost);
    costs[eId] = cost;
    previous[eId] = nodeId;
    frontier.Remove(e);
    frontier.Add(child);
}
```

How it works...

The A*mbush algorithm analyzes the path of every agent and increases the cost of that node. When an agent computes its path using A*, it is better to choose a different route than the one chosen by other agents, thus creating the sense of an ambush among the target positions.

There's more...

There is an easy-to-implement improvement over the algorithm, which leads to the P-A*mbush variation. Simply order the lurkers' list, from the closest to the farthest, and we should have a better result at almost no extra cost in computation. This is due to the fact that the ordering operation is handled just once, and could be easily implemented via a priority queue, retrieving it as a list to the main A*mbush algorithm with no additional changes.

Analyzing waypoints by height

This recipe lets us evaluate a waypoint according to its position. Strategically speaking, lower positions are at a disadvantage. In this case, we will use a flexible algorithm to get the quality of a waypoint, given the heights of its surroundings.

Getting ready

This recipe is simple enough, so there is no extra content to be aware of. The algorithm is flexible enough to receive a list of positions, which is given by the waypoints' neighbors or just the complete graph of waypoints. The surrounding's heuristic is kept outside for our perusal and it provides the game's specific design.

How to do it...

We will implement a function to evaluate a location given its height and surrounding points:

1. Declare the function for evaluating the quality:

```
public static float GetHeightQuality (Vector3 location, Vector3[]
surroundings)
```

```
{
    // next steps
}
```

2. Initialize the variables for handling the computation:

```
float maxQuality = 1f;
float minQuality = -1f;
float minHeight = Mathf.Infinity;
float maxHeight = Mathf.NegativeInfinity;
float height = location.y;
```

3. Traverse the surroundings in order to find the maximum and minimum heights:

```
foreach (Vector3 s in surroundings)
{
    if (s.y > maxHeight)
        maxHeight = s.y;
    if (s.y < minHeight)
        minHeight = s.y;
}
```

4. Compute the quality in the given range:

```
float quality = (height-minHeight) / (maxHeight - minHeight);
quality *= (maxQuality - minQuality);
quality += minQuality;
return quality;
```

How it works...

We traverse the list of surroundings to find the maximum and minimum width and then compute the location value in the range of -1 to 1. We could change this range to meet our game's design, or invert the importance of the height in the formula.

Analyzing waypoints by cover and visibility

When dealing with military games, especially FPSes, we need to define a waypoint value, by its capacity, to be a good cover point with maximum visibility for shooting or reaching other enemies visually. This recipe helps us to compute the waypoint's value given these parameters.

Getting ready

We need to create a function for checking whether a position is in the same room as the others:

```
public bool IsInSameRoom(Vector3 from, Vector3 location, string tagWall =
"Wall")
{
    RaycastHit[] hits;
    Vector3 direction = location - from;
    float rayLength = direction.magnitude;
    direction.Normalize();
    Ray ray = new Ray(from, direction);
    hits = Physics.RaycastAll(ray, rayLength);
    foreach (RaycastHit h in hits)
    {
        string tagObj = h.collider.gameObject.tag;
        if (tagObj.Equals(tagWall))
            return false;
    }
    return true;
}
```

How to do it...

We will create the function that computes the quality of the waypoint:

1. Define the function with its parameters:

   ```
   public static float GetCoverQuality(
           Vector3 location,
           int iterations,
           Vector3 characterSize,
           float radius,
           float randomRadius,
           float deltaAngle)
   {
       // next steps
   }
   ```

2. Initialize the variable for handling the degrees of rotation, possible hits received, and valid visibility:

   ```
   float theta = 0f;
   int hits = 0;
   int valid = 0;
   ```

3. Start the main loop for the iterations to be computed on this waypoint and return the computed value:

```
for (int i = 0; i < iterations; i++)
{
    // next steps
}
return (float)(hits / valid);
```

4. Create a random position near the waypoint's origin to see whether the waypoint is easily reachable:

```
Vector3 from = location;
float randomBinomial = Random.Range(-1f, 1f);
from.x += radius * Mathf.Cos(theta) + randomBinomial *
randomRadius;
from.y += Random.value * 2f * randomRadius;
from.z += radius * Mathf.Sin(theta) + randomBinomial *
randomRadius;
```

5. Check whether the random position is in the same room:

```
if (!IsInSameRoom(from, location))
    continue;
valid++;
```

6. Compute a position, about the size of our template character, around the waypoint:

```
Vector3 to = location;
to.x += Random.Range(-1f, 1f) * characterSize.x;
to.y += Random.value * characterSize.y;
to.z += Random.Range(-1f, 1f) * characterSize.z;
```

7. Cast a ray to the visibility value to check whether such a character will be visible:

```
Vector3 direction = to - location;
float distance = direction.magnitude;
direction.Normalize();
Ray ray = new Ray(location, direction);
if (Physics.Raycast(ray, distance))
    hits++;
theta = Mathf.Deg2Rad * deltaAngle;
```

How it works...

We create a number of iterations and then start putting random numbers around the waypoint to verify that it is reachable and hittable. After that, we compute a coefficient to determine its quality.

Creating waypoints automatically

Most of the time, waypoints are assigned manually by the game designer, but what happens if the level has been generated procedurally? We need to come up with an automated solution for our agents.

In this recipe, we will learn a technique called condensation that helps us deal with this problem, allowing the waypoints to compete with each other given their assigned values, meaning the relevant ones will prevail.

Getting ready

We will deal with static member functions. It is important that we know the use and value of static functions.

How to do it...

We will create the `Waypoint` class and add the methods for condensing the set of waypoints:

1. Create the `Waypoint` class, deriving from both `MonoBehaviour` and from the `IComparer` interface:

```
using UnityEngine;
using System.Collections;
using System.Collections.Generic;

public class Waypoint : MonoBehaviour, IComparer
{
  public float value;
  public List<Waypoint> neighbours;
}
```

2. Implement the `Compare` function from the interface:

```
public int Compare(object a, object b)
{
  Waypoint wa = (Waypoint)a;
  Waypoint wb = (Waypoint)b;
  if (wa.value == wb.value)
    return 0;
  if (wa.value < wb.value)
    return -1;
  return 1;
}
```

3. Implement the `static` function that checks whether an agent is able to reach one waypoint from the other:

```
public static bool CanMove(Waypoint a, Waypoint b)
{
  // implement your own behaviour for
  // deciding whether an agent can move
  // easily between two waypoints
  return true;
}
```

4. Define the member function for condensing the waypoints:

```
public static void CondenseWaypoints(List<Waypoint> waypoints,
float distanceWeight)
{
  // next steps
}
```

5. Initialize the required variables and sort the waypoints in descending order:

```
distanceWeight *= distanceWeight;
waypoints.Sort();
waypoints.Reverse();
List<Waypoint> neighbours;
```

6. Start the loop for processing each waypoint:

```
foreach (Waypoint current in waypoints)
{
  // next steps
}
```

7. Retrieve the waypoint neighbors, sort them, and start the loop for making them compete:

```
neighbours = new List<Waypoint>(current.neighbours);
neighbours.Sort();
foreach (Waypoint target in neighbours)
{
  if (target.value > current.value)
    break;
  if (!CanMove(current, target))
    continue;
  // next steps
}
```

8. Compute the target's position:

```
Vector3 deltaPos = current.transform.position;
deltaPos -= target.transform.position;
deltaPos = Vector3.Cross(deltaPos, deltaPos);
deltaPos *= distanceWeight;
```

9. Compute the target's overall value and decide whether it's worth keeping:

```
float deltaVal = current.value - target.value;
deltaVal *= deltaVal;
if (deltaVal < distanceWeight)
{
  neighbours.Remove(target);
  waypoints.Remove(target);
}
```

How it works...

We assign the `Waypoint` component to every node of the graph, or every node that is worth taking as a waypoint (because the condensation algorithm emphasizes performance).

The waypoints are ordered according to their relevance (such as the height to be used as a sniping or advantage location), and then their neighbors are checked to see which ones are going to be dismissed from the condensation. Naturally, the less valuable waypoints are kept to the end of the computation cycle.

There's more...

In the current implementation, the value member variable is an oversimplification. We know we could have several member variables with fuzzy values to determine diverse relevance points for every waypoint.

In that case, it's a good idea to synthesize all those calculations in an overall value, as presented here, or work in a better heuristic for determining the relevance of a waypoint over the others in the `Compare` implementation, so the sorting algorithm can work as expected.

See also

For further information on how to evaluate waypoints, please refer to the following recipes in this chapter:

- *Analyzing waypoints by height*
- *Analyzing waypoints by cover and visibility*

Exemplifying waypoints for decision making

Just as we learned in `Chapter 3`, *Decision Making*, evaluating a waypoint's value it is not flexible enough, but rather a more complex process. In this case, the solution is to apply techniques learned previously and incorporate them into the waypoint for tackling the problem.

The key idea behind this recipe is to add a condition to the node so that it can be evaluated, for example, using a decision tree and develop more complex heuristics for computing a waypoint's value.

Getting ready

It is important to read the recipe *Implementing a finite-state machine*, in `Chapter 3`, *Decision Making*, before diving in.

How to do it...

We will make a little adjustment to the `Waypoint` class:

1. Add a member variable to the `Waypoint` class:

   ```
   public Condition condition;
   ```

2. Assign the condition class to be used, for example `ConditionFloat`:

   ```
   condition = new ConditionFloat();
   ```

How it works...

The pseudo-abstract class `Condition`, which we learned about previously, has a member function called `Test`. This function evaluates whether a condition is met.

See also

For further information on decision making and conditions, please refer to the following recipe:

* `Chapter 3`, *Decision Making, Implementing a finite-state machine.*

Implementing influence maps

Another way to use graphs is to represent how much reach or influence an agent, or, in this case, a unit, has over an area of the world. In this context, influence is represented as the total area of a map covered by an agent, or a group of agents from the same party.

This is a key element for creating good AI decision mechanisms based on top of military presence in real-time simulation games, or games where it is important to know how much of the world is taken up by a group of agents, each representing a given faction.

Getting ready

This is a recipe that requires experience of graph building, so it is based on the general `Graph` class. That means that we will need to use a specific graph definition (no matter which one you prefer), or define our own methods to handle vertices and the neighbors' retrieval logic, as learned in `Chapter 2`, *Navigation*.

We will learn how to implement the specific algorithms for this recipe, which are based on top of the `Graph` class general functions and the `Vertex` class.

Finally, we will need a base Unity component for our agent and `Faction` enum.

The following is the code for the `Faction` enum and `Unit` classes. They can be written in the same file, which is called `Unit.cs`:

```
using UnityEngine;
using System.Collections;

public enum Faction
{
    // example values
    BLUE, RED
}

public class Unit : MonoBehaviour
{
    public Faction faction;
    public int radius = 1;
    public float influence = 1f;

    public virtual float GetDropOff(int locationDistance)
    {
        return influence;
    }
}
```

How to do it...

We will build the `VertexInfluence` and `InfluenceMap` classes, which are used for handling vertices and the graph, respectively:

1. Create the `VertexInfluence` class, deriving from `Vertex`:

```
using UnityEngine;
using System.Collections;
```

```
using System.Collections.Generic;

public class VertexInfluence : Vertex
{
    public Faction faction;
    public float value = 0f;
}
```

2. Implement the function for setting up values (it returns true if it was a success, and false otherwise):

```
public bool SetValue(Faction f, float v)
{
    bool isUpdated = false;
    if (v > value)
    {
        value = v;
        faction = f;
        isUpdated = true;
    }
    return isUpdated;
}
```

3. Create the `InfluenceMap` class deriving from `Graph` (or a more specific graph implementation):

```
using UnityEngine;
using System.Collections.Generic;

public class InfluenceMap : Graph
{
    public List<Unit> unitList;
    // works as vertices in regular graph
    GameObject[] locations;
}
```

4. Define the `Awake` function for initialization:

```
void Awake()
{
    if (unitList == null)
        unitList = new List<Unit>();
}
```

5. Implement the function for adding a unit on the map:

```
public void AddUnit(Unit u)
{
    if (unitList.Contains(u))
        return;
    unitList.Add(u);
}
```

6. Implement the function for removing a unit from the map:

```
public void RemoveUnit(Unit u)
{
    unitList.Remove(u);
}
```

7. Start building the function for computing the influence:

```
public void ComputeInfluenceSimple()
{
    VertexInfluence v;
    float dropOff;
    List<Vertex> pending = new List<Vertex>();
    List<Vertex> visited = new List<Vertex>();
    List<Vertex> frontier;
    Vertex[] neighbours;

    // next steps
}
```

8. Continue by creating a loop for iterating over the list of units:

```
foreach(Unit u in unitList)
{
    Vector3 uPos = u.transform.position;
    Vertex vert = GetNearestVertex(uPos);
    pending.Add(vert);
    // next step
}
```

9. Finally, apply BFS-based code for spreading influence given the radius reach:

```
// BFS for assigning influence
for (int i = 1; i <= u.radius; i++)
{
    frontier = new List<Vertex>();
    foreach (Vertex p in pending)
    {
```

```
        if (visited.Contains(p))
            continue;
        visited.Add(p);
        v = p as VertexInfluence;
        dropOff = u.GetDropOff(i);
        v.SetValue(u.faction, dropOff);
        neighbours = GetNeighbours(vert);
        frontier.AddRange(neighbours);
    }
    pending = new List<Vertex>(frontier);
}
```

How it works...

The influence map graph works exactly as a general graph, as well as the influence-based vertex, because there are just a couple of extra parameters for mapping the influence across the graph. The most relevant part relies on the computation of the influence, and it is based on the BFS algorithm.

For each unit on the map, we spread its influence given the radius. When the computed influence (drop-off) is greater than the vertex original faction, the vertex faction is changed.

There's more...

The drop-off function should be tuned according to your specific game needs. We can define a smarter function with the following example code, using the `locationDistance` parameter:

```
public virtual float GetDropOff(int locationDistance)
{
    float d = influence / radius * locationDistance;
    return influence - d;
}
```

It is important to note that the `locationDistance` parameter is an integer indicating the distance measured in vertices.

Finally, we could avoid using factions and instead use a reference to the unit itself. That way, we could map the influence based on individual units, but we think it makes the most sense when thinking in terms of factions or teams.

See also

- Chapter 2, *Navigation,* and the *Representing the world with grids* and *Finding the shortest path in a grid with BFS* recipes

Improving influence with map flooding

The previous influence computation is good when dealing with simple influence that is based on individual units helping a faction. However, this could lead to holes in the map instead of covering a whole section. One technique to approach that problem is flooding; it's a technique based on Dijkstra's algorithm.

Getting ready

In this recipe, we will combine two concepts into a class. First, tagging a vertex to represent that fact that it's owned by a faction; second, the drop-off function from units. Such a class is called `Guild`. This is a component to be attached to the game object; one component for each desired guild:

```
using UnityEngine;
using System;
using System.Collections;

public class Guild : MonoBehaviour
{
    public string guildName;
    public int maxStrength;
    public GameObject baseObject;
    [HideInInspector]
    public int strenghth

    public virtual void Awake()
    {
        strength = maxStrength;
    }
}
```

It also needs a drop-off function. This time, however, we wanted to create an example using Euclidean distance:

```
public virtual float GetDropOff(float distance)
{
    float d = Mathf.Pow(1 + distance, 2f);
    return strenght / d;
}
```

Finally, we will need a `GuildRecord` data type for the Dijkstra algorithm's representation of a node:

1. Create the `GuildRecord` struct, deriving from the `IComparable` interface:

    ```
    using UnityEngine;
    using System.Collections;
    using System;

    public struct GuildRecord : IComparable<GuildRecord>
    {
        public Vertex location;
        public float strength;
        public Guild guild;
    }
    ```

2. Implement the `Equal` functions:

    ```
    public override bool Equals(object obj)
    {
        GuildRecord other = (GuildRecord)obj;
        return location == other.location;
    }

    public bool Equals(GuildRecord o)
    {
        return location == o.location;
    }
    ```

3. Implement the required `IComparable` functions:

    ```
    public override int GetHashCode()
    {
        return base.GetHashCode();
    }

    public int CompareTo(GuildRecord other)
    {
        if (location == other.location)
    ```

```
        return 0;
    // the substraction is inverse for
    // having a descending binary heap
    return (int)(other.strength - strength);
}
```

How to do it...

Now, we just need to modify some files and add functionalities:

1. Include the `guild` member in the `VertexInfluence` class:

   ```
   public Guild guild;
   ```

2. Include new members in the `InfluenceMap` class:

   ```
   public float dropOffThreshold;
   private  Guild[] guildList;
   ```

3. Also, in `InfluenceMap`, add the following line to the `Awake` function:

   ```
   guildList = gameObject.GetComponents<Guild>();
   ```

4. Create the map flooding function:

   ```
   public List<GuildRecord> ComputeMapFlooding()
   {
   }
   ```

5. Declare the principal necessary variables:

   ```
   GPWiki.BinaryHeap<GuildRecord> open;
   open = new GPWiki.BinaryHeap<GuildRecord>();
   List<GuildRecord> closed;
   closed = new List<GuildRecord>();
   ```

6. Add the initial nodes for each guild in the priority queue:

   ```
   foreach (Guild g in guildList)
   {
       GuildRecord gr = new GuildRecord();
       gr.location = GetNearestVertex(g.baseObject);
       gr.guild = g;
       gr.strength = g.GetDropOff(0f);
       open.Add(gr);
   }
   ```

7. Create the main Dijkstra iteration and return the assignments:

```
while (open.Count != 0)
{
    // next steps here
}
return closed;
```

8. Take the first node in the queue and get its neighbors:

```
GuildRecord current;
current = open.Remove();
GameObject currObj;
currObj = GetVertexObj(current.location);
Vector3 currPos;
currPos = currObj.transform.position;
List<int> neighbours;
neighbours = GetNeighbors(current.location);
```

9. Create the loop for computing each neighbor, and put the current node in the closed list:

```
foreach (int n in neighbours)
{
    // next steps here
}
closed.Add(current);
```

10. Compute the drop-off from the current vertex, and check whether it is worth trying to change the guild assigned:

```
GameObject nObj = GetVertexObj(n);
Vector3 nPos = nObj.transform.position;
float dist = Vector3.Distance(currPos, nPos);
float strength = current.guild.GetDropOff(dist);
if (strength < dropOffThreshold)
    continue;
```

11. Create an auxiliary `GuildRecord` node with the current vertex's data:

```
GuildRecord neighGR = new GuildRecord();
neighGR.location = n;
neighGR.strength = strength;
VertexInfluence vi;
vi = nObj.GetComponent<VertexInfluence>();
neighGR.guild = vi.guild;
```

12. Check the closed list and validate the time when a new assignment must be avoided:

```
if (closed.Contains(neighGR))
{
    int location = neighGR.location;
    int index = closed.FindIndex(x => x.location == location);
    GuildRecord gr = closed[index];
    if (gr.guild.name != current.guild.name
            && gr.strength < strength)
        continue;
}
```

13. Check the priority queue for the same reasons:

```
else if (open.Contains(neighGR))
{
    bool mustContinue = false;
    foreach (GuildRecord gr in open)
    {
        if (gr.Equals(neighGR))
        {
            mustContinue = true;
            break;
        }
    }
    if (mustContinue)
        continue;
}
```

14. Create a new `GuildRecord` assignment and add it to the priority queue when everything else fails:

```
else
{
    neighGR = new GuildRecord();
    neighGR.location = n;
}
neighGR.guild = current.guild;
neighGR.strength = strength;
```

15. Add it to the priority queue if necessary:

```
open.Add(neighGR);
```

How it works...

The algorithm traverses the whole graph, starting from the guilds' positions. Given our previous inverse subtraction, the priority queue always starts from the strongest node and computes the assignment until it reaches a value below the `dropOffThreshold`. It also checks for ways to avoid a new assignment if the conditions are not met, if the vertex value is greater than the current strength, or if the guild assignment is the same.

See also

- The *Introducing influence maps* recipe
- `Chapter 2`, *Navigation*, and the *Finding the shortest path with Dijkstra* recipe

Improving influence with convolution filters

Convolution filters are usually applied in image processing software, but we can use the same principles to change a grid's influence given a unit's value and its surroundings. In this recipe, we will look at a couple of algorithms to modify a grid using matrix filters.

Getting ready

It is important to have grasped the concept of an influence map before implementing this recipe so that you can understand the context in which it is applied.

How to do it...

We will implement the `Convolve` function:

1. Declare the `Convolve` function:

```
public static void Convolve(
        float[,] matrix,
        ref float[,] source,
        ref float[,] destination)
{
    // next steps
}
```

2. Initialize the variables for handling the computations and the traversal of arrays:

```
int matrixLength = matrix.GetLength(0);
int size = (int)(matrixLength - 1) / 2;
int height = source.GetLength(0);
int width = source.GetLength(1);
int I, j, k, m;
```

3. Create the first loop for iterating over the destination and source grids:

```
for (i = 0; i < width-- size; i++)
{
    for (j = 0; j < height-- size; j++)
    {
        // next steps
    }
}
```

4. Implement the second loop for iterating over the filter matrix:

```
destination[i, j] = 0f;
for (k = 0; k < matrixLength; k++)
{
    for (m = 0; m < matrixLength; m++)
    {
        int row = i + k-- size;
        int col = j + m-- size;
        float aux = source[row, col] * matrix[k,m];
        destination[i, j] += aux;
    }
}
```

How it works...

We create a new grid to be swapped with the original source grid following the application of the matrix filter on each position. Then, we iterate over each position that is to be created as a destination grid and compute its result, taking the original grid's value and applying the matrix filter to it.

It is important to note that the matrix filter must be an odd-square array for the algorithm to work as expected.

There's more...

The following `ConvolveDriver` function helps us iterate using the `Convolve` function implemented previously:

1. Declare the `ConvolveDriver` function:

```
public static void ConvolveDriver(
        float[,] matrix,
        ref float[,] source,
        ref float[,] destination,
        int iterations)
{
    // next steps
}
```

2. Create the auxiliary variables for holding the grids:

```
float[,] map1;
float[,] map2;
int i;
```

3. Swap the maps, regardless of whether iterations are odd or even:

```
if (iterations % 2 == 0)
{
    map1 = source;
    map2 = destination;
}
else
{
    destination = source;
    map1 = destination;
    map2 = source;
}
```

4. Apply the previous function during the iterations and swap the maps:

```
for (i = 0; i < iterations; i++)
{
    Convolve(matrix, ref source, ref destination);
    float[,] aux = map1;
    map1 = map2;
    map2 = aux;
}
```

See also

- The *Introducing influence maps* recipe

Building a fighting circle

This recipe is based on the Kung-Fu Circle algorithm devised for the game *Kingdoms of Amalur: Reckoning*. Its purpose is to offer an intelligent way for enemies to approach a given player and set attacks on it. It is very similar to the formation recipe, but it uses a stage manager that handles approach and attack permissions based on enemy weights and attack weights. It is also implemented so that the manager is capable of handling a list of fighting circles; this is especially aimed at multiplayer games.

Getting ready

Before implementing the fighting circle algorithm, it is important to create some components that accompany the technique. First, the `Attack` class is a pseudo-abstract class for creating general-purpose attacks for each enemy, and it works as a template for the custom attacks in our game. Second, we need the `Enemy` class, which is the holder of the enemy's logic and requests. As we will see, the `Enemy` class holds a list of the different attack components found in the game object.

The code for the `Attack` class is as follows:

```
using UnityEngine;
using System.Collections;

public class Attack : MonoBehaviour
{
    public int weight;

    public virtual IEnumerator Execute()
    {
        // your attack behaviour here
        yield break;
    }
}
```

The steps to build the Enemy component are as follows:

1. Create the Enemy class:

```
using UnityEngine;
using System.Collections;

public class Enemy : MonoBehaviour
{
    public StageManager stageManager;
    public int slotWeight;
    [HideInInspector]
    public int circleId = -1;
    [HideInInspector]
    public bool isAssigned;
    [HideInInspector]
    public bool isAttacking;
    [HideInInspector]
    public Attack[] attackList;
}
```

2. Implement the Start function:

```
void Start()
{
    attackList = gameObject.GetComponents<Attack>();
}
```

3. Implement the function for assigning a target fighting circle:

```
public void SetCircle(GameObject circleObj = null)
{
    int id = -1;
    if (circleObj == null)
    {
        Vector3 position = transform.position;
        id = stageManager.GetClosestCircle(position);
    }
    else
    {
        FightingCircle fc;
        fc = circleObj.GetComponent<FightingCircle>();
        if (fc != null)
            id = fc.gameObject.GetInstanceID();
    }
    circleId = id;
}
```

4. Define the function for requesting a slot from the manager:

```
public bool RequestSlot()
{
    isAssigned = stageManager.GrantSlot(circleId, this);
    return isAssigned;
}
```

5. Define the function for releasing a slot from the manager:

```
public void ReleaseSlot()
{
    stageManager.ReleaseSlot(circleId, this);
    isAssigned = false;
    circleId = -1;
}
```

6. Implement the function for requesting an attack from the list (the order is the same as in the inspector):

```
public bool RequestAttack(int id)
{
    return stageManager.GrantAttack(circleId, attackList[id]);
}
```

7. Define the virtual function for the attack behavior:

```
public virtual IEnumerator Attack()
{
    // TODO
    // your attack behaviour here
    yield break;
}
```

How to do it...

Now, we implement the `FightingCircle` and `StageManager` classes:

1. Create the `FightingCircle` class along with its member variables:

```
using UnityEngine;
using System.Collections;
using System.Collections.Generic;

public class FightingCircle : MonoBehaviour
{
```

```
        public int slotCapacity;
        public int attackCapacity;
        public float attackRadius;
        public GameObject player;
        [HideInInspector]
        public int slotsAvailable;
        [HideInInspector]
        public int attackAvailable;
        [HideInInspector]
        public List<GameObject> enemyList;
        [HideInInspector]
        public Dictionary<int, Vector3> posDict;
    }
```

2. Implement the `Awake` function for initialization:

```
    void Awake()
    {
        slotsAvailable = slotCapacity;
        attackAvailable = attackCapacity;
        enemyList = new List<GameObject>();
        posDict = new Dictionary<int, Vector3>();
        if (player == null)
            player = gameObject;
    }
```

3. Define the `Update` function so that the slots' positions get updated:

```
    void Update()
    {
        if (enemyList.Count == 0)
            return;
        Vector3 anchor = player.transform.position;
        int i;
        for (i = 0; i < enemyList.Count; i++)
        {
            Vector3 position = anchor;
            Vector3 slotPos = GetSlotLocation(i);
            int enemyId = enemyList[i].GetInstanceID();
            position += player.transform.TransformDirection(slotPos);
            posDict[enemyId] = position;
        }
    }
```

4. Implement the function for adding enemies to the circle:

```
public bool AddEnemy(GameObject enemyObj)
{
    Enemy enemy = enemyObj.GetComponent<Enemy>();
    int enemyId = enemyObj.GetInstanceID();
    if (slotsAvailable < enemy.slotWeight)
        return false;
    enemyList.Add(enemyObj);
    posDict.Add(enemyId, Vector3.zero);
    slotsAvailable -= enemy.slotWeight;
    return true;
}
```

5. Implement the function for removing enemies from the circle:

```
public bool RemoveEnemy(GameObject enemyObj)
{
    bool isRemoved = enemyList.Remove(enemyObj);
    if (isRemoved)
    {
        int enemyId = enemyObj.GetInstanceID();
        posDict.Remove(enemyId);
        Enemy enemy = enemyObj.GetComponent<Enemy>();
        slotsAvailable += enemy.slotWeight;
    }
    return isRemoved;
}
```

6. Implement the function for swapping enemies' positions in the circle:

```
public void SwapEnemies(GameObject enemyObjA, GameObject enemyObjB)
{
    int indexA = enemyList.IndexOf(enemyObjA);
    int indexB = enemyList.IndexOf(enemyObjB);
    if (indexA != -1 && indexB != -1)
    {
        enemyList[indexB] = enemyObjA;
        enemyList[indexA] = enemyObjB;
    }
}
```

7. Define the function for getting an enemy's spatial position according to the circle:

```
public Vector3? GetPositions(GameObject enemyObj)
{
    int enemyId = enemyObj.GetInstanceID();
    if (!posDict.ContainsKey(enemyId))
```

```
        return null;
    return posDict[enemyId];
}
```

8. Implement the function for computing the spatial location of a slot:

```
private Vector3 GetSlotLocation(int slot)
{
    Vector3 location = new Vector3();
    float degrees = 360f / enemyList.Count;
    degrees *= (float)slot;
    location.x = Mathf.Cos(Mathf.Deg2Rad * degrees);
    location.x *= attackRadius;
    location.z = Mathf.Cos(Mathf.Deg2Rad * degrees);
    location.z *= attackRadius;
    return location;
}
```

9. Implement the function for virtually adding attacks to the circle:

```
public bool AddAttack(int weight)
{
    if (attackAvailable - weight < 0)
        return false;
    attackAvailable -= weight;
    return true;
}
```

10. Define the function for virtually releasing the attacks from the circle:

```
public void ResetAttack()
{
    attackAvailable = attackCapacity;
}
```

11. Now create the `StageManager` class:

```
using UnityEngine;
using System.Collections;
using System.Collections.Generic;

public class StageManager : MonoBehaviour
{
    public List<FightingCircle> circleList;
    private Dictionary<int, FightingCircle> circleDic;
    private Dictionary<int, List<Attack>> attackRqsts;
}
```

12. Implement the `Awake` function for initialization:

```
void Awake()
{
    circleList = new List<FightingCircle>();
    circleDic = new Dictionary<int, FightingCircle>();
    attackRqsts = new Dictionary<int, List<Attack>>();
    foreach(FightingCircle fc in circleList)
    {
        AddCircle(fc);
    }
}
```

13. Create the function for adding circles to the manager:

```
public void AddCircle(FightingCircle circle)
{
    if (!circleList.Contains(circle))
        return;
    circleList.Add(circle);
    int objId = circle.gameObject.GetInstanceID();
    circleDic.Add(objId, circle);
    attackRqsts.Add(objId, new List<Attack>());
}
```

14. Also, create the function for removing circles from the manager:

```
public void RemoveCircle(FightingCircle circle)
{
    bool isRemoved = circleList.Remove(circle);
    if (!isRemoved)
        return;
    int objId = circle.gameObject.GetInstanceID();
    circleDic.Remove(objId);
    attackRqsts[objId].Clear();
    attackRqsts.Remove(objId);
}
```

15. Define the function for getting the closest circle if given a position:

```
public int GetClosestCircle(Vector3 position)
{
    FightingCircle circle = null;
    float minDist = Mathf.Infinity;
    foreach(FightingCircle c in circleList)
    {
        Vector3 circlePos = c.transform.position;
        float dist = Vector3.Distance(position, circlePos);
```

```
        if (dist < minDist)
        {
            minDist = dist;
            circle = c;
        }
    }
    return circle.gameObject.GetInstanceID();
}
```

16. Define the function for granting an enemy a slot in a given circle:

```
public bool GrantSlot(int circleId, Enemy enemy)
{
    return circleDic[circleId].AddEnemy(enemy.gameObject);
}
```

17. Implement the function for releasing an enemy from a given circle ID:

```
public void ReleaseSlot(int circleId, Enemy enemy)
{
    circleDic[circleId].RemoveEnemy(enemy.gameObject);
}
```

18. Define the function for granting attack permissions and adding them to the manager:

```
public bool GrantAttack(int circleId, Attack attack)
{
    bool answer = circleDic[circleId].AddAttack(attack.weight);
    attackRqsts[circleId].Add(attack);
    return answer;
}
```

19. Implement the function for executing all the queued attacks:

```
public IEnumerator ExecuteAtacks()
{
    foreach (int circle in attackRqsts.Keys)
    {
        List<Attack> attacks = attackRqsts[circle];
        foreach (Attack a in attacks)
            yield return a.Execute();
    }
    foreach (FightingCircle fc in circleList)
        fc.ResetAttack();
}
```

How it works...

The `Attack` and `Enemy` classes control the behaviors when needed, so the `Enemy` class can be called from another component in the game object. The `FightingCircle` class is very similar to `FormationPattern`, in that it computes the target positions for a given enemy. It just does it in a slightly different way. Finally, the `StageManager` grants all the necessary permissions for assigning and releasing enemy and attack slots for each circle.

There's more...

It is worth noting that the fighting circle can be added as a component of a game object that works as the target player itself, or a different empty object that holds a reference to the player's game object.

Also, you could move the functions for granting and executing attacks to the fighting circle. We wanted to keep them in the manager so that the attacks' executions are centralized, and the circles just work for handling target positions; just like formations.

See also

For further information, please refer to the following material:

- Refer to the *Handling formations* recipe
- For further information on the Kung-Fu Circle algorithm, please refer to the book *Game AI Pro*, by Steve Rabin

Agent Awareness

6

In this chapter, we will learn some algorithm recipes for simulating senses and agent awareness:

- The seeing function using a collider-based system
- The hearing function using a collider-based system
- The smelling function using a collider-based system
- The seeing function using a graph-based system
- The hearing function using a graph-based system
- The smelling function using a graph-based system
- Creating awareness in a stealth game

Introduction

In this chapter, we will learn different approaches to simulating sense stimuli on an agent. We will learn how to use tools that we are already familiar with to create these simulations, colliders, and graphs.

In the first approach, we will take advantage of ray casting, colliders, and the `MonoBehaviour` functions bound to this component, such as `OnCollisionEnter`, in order to leverage the need to acquire objects nearby in the three-dimensional world. Then, we will learn how to simulate the same stimuli using the graph theory and functions so that we can take advantage of this way of representing the world.

Finally, we'll learn how to implement agent awareness using a mixed approach that considers the previously learned sensory-level algorithms.

The seeing function using a collider-based system

This is probably the easiest way to simulate vision. We take a collider, be it a mesh or a Unity primitive, and use it as the tool for determining whether or not an object is inside the agent's vision range.

Getting ready

It's important to have a collider component attached to the same game object using the script in this recipe, as well as the other collider-based algorithms in this chapter. In this case, it's recommended that the collider is a pyramid-based one in order to simulate a vision cone. The fewer the polygons, the faster it will be in the game.

How to do it...

We will create a component that is able to see enemies nearby:

1. Create the `Visor` component, declaring its member variables. It is important to add the following corresponding tags to Unity's configuration:

```
using UnityEngine;
using System.Collections;

public class Visor : MonoBehaviour
{
    public string tagWall = "Wall";
    public string tagTarget = "Enemy";
    public GameObject agent;
}
```

2. Implement the function for initializing the game object in case the component is already assigned to it:

```
void Start()
{
    if (agent == null)
        agent = gameObject;
}
```

3. Declare the function for checking collisions in every frame:

```
public void OnTriggerStay(Collider coll)
{
    // next steps here
}
```

4. Discard the collision if it is not a target:

```
string tag = coll.gameObject.tag;
if (!tag.Equals(tagTarget))
    return;
```

5. Get the game object's position and compute its direction from the visor:

```
GameObject target = coll.gameObject;
Vector3 agentPos = agent.transform.position;
Vector3 targetPos = target.transform.position;
Vector3 direction = targetPos - agentPos;
```

6. Compute its length and create a new ray to be shot soon:

```
float length = direction.magnitude;
direction.Normalize();
Ray ray = new Ray(agentPos, direction);
```

7. Cast the ray created and retrieve all the hits:

```
RaycastHit[] hits;
hits = Physics.RaycastAll(ray, length);
```

8. Check for any walls between the visor and target. If there are none, we can proceed to call our functions or develop the behaviors that are to be triggered:

```
int i;
for (i = 0; i < hits.Length; i++)
{
    GameObject hitObj;
    hitObj = hits[i].collider.gameObject;
    tag = hitObj.tag;
    if (tag.Equals(tagWall))
        return;
}
// TODO
// target is visible
// code your behaviour below
```

How it works...

The following diagram shows how the two-step vision system works:

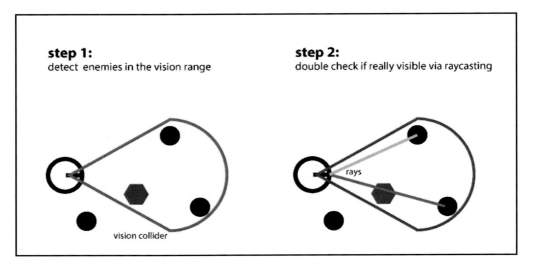

The collider component checks every frame to see whether it is colliding with any game object in the scene. We leverage the optimizations in Unity's scene graph and engine, and focus only on how to handle the valid collisions.

After checking this, if a target object is inside the vision range represented by the collider, we cast a ray in order to check whether it is really visible or whether there is a wall between the target and the agent.

The hearing function using a collider-based system

In this recipe, we will emulate a sense of hearing by developing two entities: a sound emitter and a sound receiver. It is based on the principles proposed by Millington for simulating a hearing system, and it uses the power of Unity colliders to detect receivers near an emitter.

Getting ready

As with the other recipes based on colliders, we will need collider components attached to every object that is to be checked, and rigid body components attached to either emitters or receivers.

How to do it...

We will create the `SoundReceiver` class for our agents, and `SoundEmitter` for things such as alarms:

1. Create the class for the sound-receiver object:

   ```
   using UnityEngine;
   using System.Collections;

   public class SoundReceiver : MonoBehaviour
   {
       public float soundThreshold;
   }
   ```

2. Define the function for the behavior that is handling the reception of sound:

   ```
   public virtual void Receive(float intensity, Vector3 position)
   {
       // TODO
       // code your own behaviour here
   }
   ```

3. Now, let's create the class for the sound-emitter object:

   ```
   using UnityEngine;
   using System.Collections;
   using System.Collections.Generic;

   public class SoundEmitter : MonoBehaviour
   {
       public float soundIntensity;
       public float soundAttenuation;
       public GameObject emitterObject;
       private Dictionary<int, SoundReceiver> receiverDic;
   }
   ```

4. Initialize the list of receivers nearby and the emitter object, in case the component is attached directly:

```
void Start()
{
    receiverDic = new Dictionary<int, SoundReceiver>();
    if (emitterObject == null)
        emitterObject = gameObject;
}
```

5. Implement the function for adding new receivers to the list when they enter the emitter bounds:

```
public void OnTriggerEnter(Collider coll)
{
    SoundReceiver receiver;
    receiver = coll.gameObject.GetComponent<SoundReceiver>();
    if (receiver == null)
        return;
    int objId = coll.gameObject.GetInstanceID();
    receiverDic.Add(objId, receiver);
}
```

6. Also, implement the function for removing receivers from the list when they are out of reach:

```
public void OnTriggerExit(Collider coll)
{
    SoundReceiver receiver;
    receiver = coll.gameObject.GetComponent<SoundReceiver>();
    if (receiver == null)
        return;
    int objId = coll.gameObject.GetInstanceID();
    receiverDic.Remove(objId);
}
```

7. Define the function for emitting sound waves to nearby agents:

```
public void Emit()
{
    GameObject srObj;
    Vector3 srPos;
    float intensity;
    float distance;
    Vector3 emitterPos = emitterObject.transform.position;
    // next step here
}
```

8. Compute sound attenuation for every receiver:

```
foreach (SoundReceiver sr in receiverDic.Values)
{
    srObj = sr.gameObject;
    srPos = srObj.transform.position;
    distance = Vector3.Distance(srPos, emitterPos);
    intensity = soundIntensity;
    intensity -= soundAttenuation * distance;
    if (intensity < sr.soundThreshold)
        continue;
    sr.Receive(intensity, emitterPos);
}
```

How it works...

The following diagram shows how the sound emulation system works with colliders:

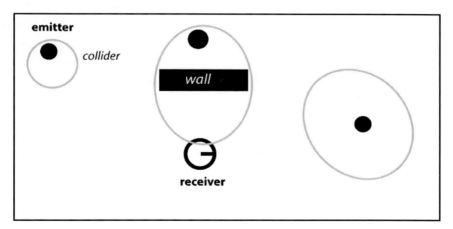

The collider triggers help to register agents in the list of agents assigned to an emitter. The sound emission function then takes into account the agent's distance from the emitter in order to decrease its intensity using the concept of sound attenuation.

There's more...

We can develop a more flexible algorithm by defining different types of walls that affect sound intensity. It works by casting rays and adding up their values to the sound attenuation:

1. Create a dictionary for storing wall types as strings (using tags) and their corresponding attenuation:

```
public Dictionary<string, float> wallTypes;
```

2. Reduce sound intensity this way:

```
intensity -= GetWallAttenuation(emitterPos, srPos);
```

3. Define the function that was called in the previous step:

```
public float GetWallAttenuation(Vector3 emitterPos, Vector3
receiverPos)
{
    // next steps here
}
```

4. Compute the necessary values for ray casting:

```
float attenuation = 0f;
Vector3 direction = receiverPos - emitterPos;
float distance = direction.magnitude;
direction.Normalize();
```

5. Cast the ray and retrieve the hits:

```
Ray ray = new Ray(emitterPos, direction);
RaycastHit[] hits = Physics.RaycastAll(ray, distance);
```

6. For every wall type found via tags, add up its value (stored in the dictionary):

```
int i;
for (i = 0; i < hits.Length; i++)
{
    GameObject obj;
    string tag;
    obj = hits[i].collider.gameObject;
    tag = obj.tag;
    if (wallTypes.ContainsKey(tag))
        attenuation += wallTypes[tag];
}
return attenuation;
```

The smelling function using a collider-based system

Smelling is one of the trickiest senses to translate from the real to the virtual world. There are several techniques, but most of them are inclined to use colliders or graph logic.

Smelling can be simulated by computing a collision between an agent and odor particles, scattered throughout the game level.

Getting ready

As with the other recipes based on colliders, we will need collider components attached to every object that is to be checked, and rigid body components attached to either emitters or receivers.

How to do it...

We will develop the scripts for representing odor particles and agents that are able to smell:

1. Create the particle's script and define its member variables for computing its lifespan:

```
using UnityEngine;
using System.Collections;

public class OdourParticle : MonoBehaviour
{
    public float timespan;
    private float timer;
}
```

2. Implement the `Start` function for proper validations:

```
void Start()
{
    if (timespan < 0f)
        timespan = 0f;
    timer = timespan;
}
```

3. Implement the `timer` and destroy the object after its life cycle ends:

```
void Update()
{
    timer -= Time.deltaTime;
    if (timer < 0f)
        Destroy(gameObject);
}
```

4. Create the class for representing the sniffer agent:

```
using UnityEngine;
using System.Collections;
using System.Collections.Generic;

public class Smeller : MonoBehaviour
{
    private Vector3 target;
    private Dictionary<int, GameObject> particles;
}
```

5. Initialize the dictionary for storing odor `particles`:

```
void Start()
{
    particles = new Dictionary<int, GameObject>();
}
```

6. Add to the dictionary the colliding objects that have the `OdourParticle` component attached:

```
public void OnTriggerEnter(Collider coll)
{
    GameObject obj = coll.gameObject;
    OdourParticle op;
    op = obj.GetComponent<OdourParticle>();
    if (op == null)
        return;
    int objId = obj.GetInstanceID();
    particles.Add(objId, obj);
    UpdateTarget();
}
```

7. Release the odor particles from the local dictionary when they are out of the agent's range or after they've been destroyed:

```
public void OnTriggerExit(Collider coll)
{
    GameObject obj = coll.gameObject;
    int objId = obj.GetInstanceID();
    bool isRemoved;
    isRemoved = particles.Remove(objId);
    if (!isRemoved)
        return;
    UpdateTarget();
}
```

8. Create the function for computing the odor `centroid` according to the current elements in the dictionary:

```
private void UpdateTarget()
{
    Vector3 centroid = Vector3.zero;
    foreach (GameObject p in particles.Values)
    {
        Vector3 pos = p.transform.position;
        centroid += pos;
    }
    target = centroid;
}
```

9. Implement the function for retrieving the odor centroids, if any:

```
public Vector3? GetTargetPosition()
{
    if (particles.Keys.Count == 0)
        return null;
    return target;
}
```

How it works...

The following diagram shows how the smell system works:

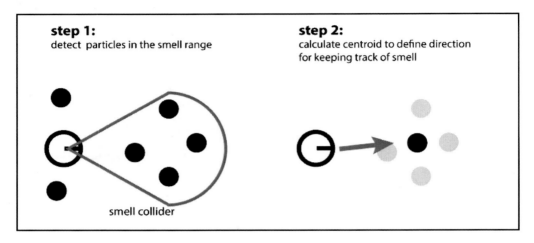

Just like the hearing recipe based on colliders, we use the trigger colliders in order to register odor particles in an agent's perception (implemented using a dictionary). When a particle is included or removed, the odor centroid is computed. However, we implement a function for retrieving that centroid because, when no odor particle is registered, the internal centroid position is not updated.

There's more...

Particle emission logic is left behind to be implemented according to our game's needs, and it's basically instantiating odor-particle prefabs. Also, it is recommended that you attach the rigid body components to the agents. Odor particles are prone to be massively instantiated, reducing the game's performance.

The seeing function using a graph-based system

We will start looking at those recipes using graph-based logic in order to simulate sense. Again, we start by developing a sense of vision.

Getting ready

It is important to have grasped `Chapter 2`, *Navigation,* in order to understand the inner workings of the graph-based recipes.

How to do it...

We will just implement a new file:

1. Create the class for handling vision:

```
using UnityEngine;
using System.Collections;
using System.Collections.Generic;

public class VisorGraph : MonoBehaviour
{
    public int visionReach;
    public GameObject visorObj;
    public Graph visionGraph;
}
```

2. Validate the visor object in case the component is not attached:

```
void Start()
{
    if (visorObj == null)
        visorObj = gameObject;
}
```

3. Define and start building the function for detecting the visibility of a given set of nodes:

```
public bool IsVisible(int[] visibilityNodes)
{
    int vision = visionReach;
    int src = visionGraph.GetNearestVertex(visorObj);
    HashSet<int> visibleNodes = new HashSet<int>();
    Queue<int> queue = new Queue<int>();
    queue.Enqueue(src);
}
```

4. Implement a **Breadth-First Search (BFS)** algorithm:

```
while (queue.Count != 0)
{
    if (vision == 0)
        break;
    int v = queue.Dequeue();
    List<int> neighbours = visionGraph.GetNeighbors(v);
    foreach (int n in neighbours)
    {
        if (visibleNodes.Contains(n))
            continue;
        queue.Enqueue(v);
        visibleNodes.Add(v);
    }
}
```

5. Compare the set of visible nodes with the set of nodes reached by the vision system:

```
foreach (int vn in visibleNodes)
{
    if (visibleNodes.Contains(vn))
        return true;
}
```

6. Return `false` if there is no match between the two sets of nodes:

```
return false;
```

How it works...

The recipe uses the BFS algorithm in order to discover nodes within its vision reach and then compares this set of nodes to the set where agents reside.

The input array is computed before being used by the algorithm and is beyond the scope of this recipe because it relies on pinpointing, for example, the position of each agent or object that needs to be checked visibly.

The hearing function using a graph-based system

Hearing works in a similar way to vision, but doesn't take into account the nodes' direct visibility because of the properties of the sound. However, we still need a sound receiver in order to make it work. Instead of making an agent a direct sound receiver, in this recipe, the sound travels along the sound graph and is perceived by the graph nodes.

Getting ready

It is important to have grasped the chapter regarding path finding in order to understand the inner workings of the graph-based recipes.

How to do it...

1. Create the emitter class:

```
using UnityEngine;
using System.Collections;
using System.Collections.Generic;

public class EmitterGraph : MonoBehaviour
{
    // next steps
}
```

2. Declare the member variables:

```
public int soundIntensity;
public Graph soundGraph;
public GameObject emitterObj;
```

3. Implement the validation of the emitter object's reference:

```
public void Start()
{
    if (emitterObj == null)
        emitterObj = gameObject;
}
```

4. Declare the function for emitting sounds:

```
public int[] Emit()
{
    // next steps
}
```

5. Declare and assign the variables needed:

```
List<int> nodeIds = new List<int>();
Queue<int> queue = new Queue<int>();
List<int> neighbours;
int intensity = soundIntensity;
int src = soundGraph.GetNearestVertex(emitterObj);
```

6. Add the source node to the list of reached nodes and the queue:

```
nodeIds.Add(src);
queue.Enqueue(src);
```

7. Code the BFS loop for reaching out to nodes:

```
while (queue.Count != 0)
{
    // next steps
}
return nodeIds.ToArray();
```

8. Finish the loop if the sound runs out of intensity:

```
if (intensity == 0)
    break;
```

9. Take a node from the queue and get its neighbors:

```
int v = queue.Dequeue();
neighbours = soundGraph.GetNeighbors(v);
```

10. Check the neighbors and add them to the queue if necessary:

```
foreach (int n in neighbours)
{
    if (nodeIds.Contains(n))
        continue;
    queue.Enqueue(n);
    nodeIds.Add(n);
}
```

11. Reduce the sound intensity:

```
intensity--;
```

How it works...

This recipe returns the list of nodes affected by sound intensity using the BFS algorithm. The algorithm stops when there are no more nodes to visit, or when the intensity of the sound is dimmed by the graph traversal.

There's more...

After learning how to implement smelling using both colliders and graph logic, you could develop a new hybrid algorithm that relies on a heuristic that takes distance as input. If a node goes beyond the sound's maximum distance, there's no need to add its neighbors to the queue.

See also

Refer to the following recipes in `Chapter 2`, *Navigation*:

- *Breadth-First Search algorithm*
- *A* algorithm (for taking a heuristic function as an argument)*

The smelling function using a graph-based system

In this recipe, we take a mixed approach to tag vertices with a given odor particle that collides with it.

Getting ready

The vertices should have a broad collider attached so that they catch the odor particles nearby.

How to do it...

1. Add the following member variable to the odor-particle script to store its parent ID:

    ```
    public int parent;
    ```

2. Create the new odor-enabled class, deriving from the original vertex:

    ```
    using UnityEngine;
    using System.Collections;
    using System.Collections.Generic;

    public class VertexOdour : Vertex
    {
        private Dictionary<int, OdourParticle> odourDic;
    }
    ```

3. Initialize the odor dictionary in the proper function:

    ```
    public void Start()
    {
        odourDic = new Dictionary<int, OdourParticle>();
    }
    ```

4. Add the odor to the vertex's dictionary:

    ```
    public void OnCollisionEnter(Collision coll)
    {
        OdourOdourParticle op;
        op = coll.gameObject.GetComponent<OdourParticle>();
        if (op == null)
            return;
        int id = op.parent;
        odourDic.Add(id, op);
    }
    ```

5. Remove the odor from the vertex's dictionary:

    ```
    public void OnCollisionExit(Collision coll)
    {
        OdourParticle op;
        op = coll.gameObject.GetComponent<OdourParticle>();
        if (op == null)
            return;
        int id = op.parent;
        odourDic.Remove(id);
    }
    ```

6. Implement the function for checking whether any odor is tagged:

```
public bool HasOdour()
{
    if (odourDic.Values.Count == 0)
        return false;
    return true;
}
```

7. Implement the function for checking whether a given type of odor is indexed in the vertex:

```
public bool OdourExists(int id)
{
    return odourDic.ContainsKey(id);
}
```

How it works...

The odor particles collide with the vertices, being indexed in their odor dictionary. From that point on, our agents can check whether a given odor is registered in a vertex nearby.

See also

- Chapter 2, *Navigation*, and the *BFS and graph construction* recipe

Creating awareness in a stealth game

Now that we know how to implement sensory-level algorithms, it's time to see how they can be taken into account in order to develop higher-level techniques for creating agent awareness.

This recipe is based on the work of Brook Miles and the team at Klei Entertainment for the game *Mark of the Ninja*. The mechanism revolves around the notion of having interest sources that can be seen or heard by the agents and a sensory manager to handle those.

Getting ready

As a lot of things revolve around the idea of interests, we'll need two data structures for defining the interests' sense and priority, and a data type for the interest itself.

This is the data structure for sense:

```
public enum InterestSense
{
    SOUND,
    SIGHT
};
```

This is the data structure for priority:

```
public enum InterestPriority
{
    LOWEST = 0,
    BROKEN = 1,
    MISSING = 2,
    SUSPECT = 4,
    SMOKE = 4,
    BOX = 5,
    DISTRACTIONFLARE = 10,
    TERROR = 20
};
```

The following is the interest data type:

```
using UnityEngine;
using System.Collections;

public struct Interest
{
    public InterestSense sense;
    public InterestPriority priority;
    public Vector3 position;
}
```

Before developing the necessary classes for implementing this idea, it's important to note that sensory-level functions are left blank in order to keep the recipe flexible and open to our custom implementations. These implementations could be developed using some of the recipes learned previously.

How to do it...

This is a long recipe where we'll implement two extensive classes. It is advised to read the
following steps carefully:

1. Let's start by creating the class that defines our agents and its member variables:

```
using UnityEngine;
using System.Collections;
using System.Collections.Generic;

public class AgentAwared : MonoBehaviour
{
    protected Interest interest;
    protected bool isUpdated = false;
}
```

2. Define the function for checking whether a given interest is relevant or not:

```
public bool IsRelevant(Interest i)
{
    int oldValue = (int)interest.priority;
    int newValue = (int)i.priority;
    if (newValue <= oldValue)
        return false;
    return true;
}
```

3. Implement the function for setting a new interest in the agent:

```
public void Notice(Interest i)
{
    StopCoroutine(Investigate());
    interest = i;
    StartCoroutine(Investigate());
}
```

4. Define the custom function for investigating. This will have our own
implementation, and it will take account of the agent's interest:

```
public virtual IEnumerator Investigate()
{
    // TODO
    // develop your implementation
    yield break;
}
```

5. Define the custom function for leading. This will define what an agent does when it's in charge of giving orders and will depend on our own implementation:

```
public virtual IEnumerator Lead()
{
    // TODO
    // develop your implementation
    yield break;
}
```

6. Create the class for defining interest sources:

```
using UnityEngine;
using System.Collections;
using System.Collections.Generic;

public class InterestSource : MonoBehaviour
{
    public InterestSense sense;
    public float radius;
    public InterestPriority priority;
    public bool isActive;
}
```

7. Implement a property for retrieving the interest value:

```
public Interest interest
{
    get
    {
        Interest i;
        i.position = transform.position;
        i.priority = priority;
        i.sense = sense;
        return i;
    }
}
```

8. Define the function for checking whether or not the agent is affected by the interest source. This could be defined in the agent's class, but it requires some changes in several of the following steps. This is one of the sensory-level functions:

```
protected bool IsAffectedSight(AgentAwared agent)
{
    // TODO
```

```
        // your sight check implementation
        return false;
}
```

9. Implement the next sensory-level function for checking whether an agent is affected by sound. It has the same architectural considerations as the previous step:

```
protected bool IsAffectedSound(AgentAwared agent)
{
    // TODO
    // your sound check implementation
    return false;
}
```

10. Define the function for getting the list of agents affected by the interest source. It is declared virtual, in case we need to specify it further or simply change the way it works:

```
public virtual List<AgentAwared> GetAffected(AgentAwared[]
agentList)
{
    List<AgentAwared> affected;
    affected = new List<AgentAwared>();
    Vector3 interPos = transform.position;
    Vector3 agentPos;
    float distance;
    // next steps
}
```

11. Start creating the main loop for traversing the list of agents and return the list of those affected:

```
foreach (AgentAwared agent in agentList)
{
    // next steps
}
return affected;
```

12. Discriminate an agent if it is beyond the source's action radius:

```
agentPos = agent.transform.position;
distance = Vector3.Distance(interPos, agentPos);
if (distance > radius)
    continue;
```

13. Check whether the agent is affected, given the source's type of sense:

```
bool isAffected = false;
switch (sense)
{
    case InterestSense.SIGHT:
        isAffected = IsAffectedSight(agent);
        break;
    case InterestSense.SOUND:
        isAffected = IsAffectedSound(agent);
        break;
}
```

14. If the agent is affected, add it to the list:

```
if (!isAffected)
    continue;
affected.Add(agent);
```

15. Next, create the class for the sensory manager:

```
using UnityEngine;
using System.Collections;
using System.Collections.Generic;

public class SensoryManager : MonoBehaviour
{
    public List<AgentAwared> agents;
    public List<InterestSource> sources;
}
```

16. Implement its `Awake` function:

```
public void Awake()
{
    agents = new List<AgentAwared>();
    sources = new List<InterestSource>();
}
```

17. Declare the function for getting a set of scouts, given a group of agents:

```
public List<AgentAwared> GetScouts(AgentAwared[] agents, int leader
= -1)
{
    // next steps
}
```

18. Validate the number of agents and return the list:

```
if (agents.Length == 0)
    return new List<AgentAwared>(0);
if (agents.Length == 1)
    return new List<AgentAwared>(agents);
```

19. Remove the leader, if given its index:

```
List<AgentAwared> agentList;
agentList = new List<AgentAwared>(agents);
if (leader > -1)
    agentList.RemoveAt(leader);
```

20. Calculate the number of scouts to retrieve:

```
List<AgentAwared> scouts;
scouts = new List<AgentAwared>();
float numAgents = (float)agents.Length;
int numScouts = (int)Mathf.Log(numAgents, 2f);
```

21. Get the random scouts from the list of agents:

```
while (numScouts != 0)
{
    int numA = agentList.Count;
    int r = Random.Range(0, numA);
    AgentAwared a = agentList[r];
    scouts.Add(a);
    agentList.RemoveAt(r);
    numScouts--;
}
```

22. Retrieve the scouts:

```
return scouts;
```

23. Define the function for checking the list of interest sources:

```
public void UpdateLoop()
{
    List<AgentAwared> affected;
    AgentAwared leader;
    List<AgentAwared> scouts;
    foreach (InterestSource source in sources)
    {
        // next steps
    }
}
```

24. Avoid inactive sources:

```
if (!source.isActive)
    continue;
source.isActive = false;
```

25. Avoid sources that don't affect any agent:

```
affected = source.GetAffected(agents.ToArray());
if (affected.Count == 0)
    continue;
```

26. Get a random `leader` and the set of `scouts`:

```
int l = Random.Range(0, affected.Count);
leader = affected[l];
scouts = GetScouts(affected.ToArray(), l);
```

27. Call the leader to its role if necessary:

```
if (leader.Equals(scouts[0]))
    StartCoroutine(leader.Lead());
```

28. Finally, inform the scouts about noticing the interest, in case it's relevant to them:

```
foreach (AgentAwared a in scouts)
{
    Interest i = source.interest;
    if (a.IsRelevant(i))
        a.Notice(i);
}
```

How it works...

There is a list of interest sources that could get the attention of a number of agents in the world. That list is kept in a manager that handles the global update for every source, taking into account just the active ones.

An interest source receives the list of agents in the world and retrieves only the affected agents after a two-step process. First, it sets aside all the agents that are outside its action radius and then only takes into account those agents that can be reached with a finer (and more expensive) sensory-level mechanism.

The manager handles the affected agents, sets up scouts and their leader, and finally informs all of them about their relevant interests.

There's more...

It is worth mentioning that the `SensoryManager` class works as a hub to store and organize the list of agents and the list of interest sources, so it ought to be a singleton. Its duplication could bring about undesired complexity or behavior.

An agent's interest is automatically changed by the sensory manager using the priority values. Still, it can be reset when needed, using the `Notice` public function.

There is room for improvement still, depending on our game. The scout lists can overlap each other, and it's up to us and our game to handle this scenario the best way we can. However, the system we built takes advantage of the priority values to make decisions.

See also

For further information on the train of thought behind this recipe, please refer to Steve Rabin's book, *Game AI Pro*.

Board Games and Applied Search AI

7

In this chapter, you will learn a family of algorithms for developing board game AI:

- Working with the game-tree class
- Implementing Minimax
- Implementing Negamax
- Implementing AB Negamax
- Implementing NegaScout
- Implementing a Tic-Tac-Toe rival
- Implementing a Checkers rival
- Implementing Rock-Paper-Scissors AI with UCB1
- Implementing Regret Matching

Introduction

In this chapter, you will learn about a family of algorithms for developing board game techniques and creating artificial intelligence. They are based on the principle of a game-tree graph that spans as we evaluate a state and decide to visit its neighbors. They also take into account board games for two rivals. But, with a little bit of work, some of them can be extended to accommodate more players.

Working with the game-tree class

The game state can be represented in a lot of different ways, but you will learn how to create extendible classes to use the high-level board AI algorithms for different circumstances.

Getting ready...

It is important to be clear on object-oriented programming, specifically on inheritance and polymorphism. This is because we'll be creating generic functions that can be applied to a number of board game decisions, and then we'll be writing specific sub-classes that inherit and further specify these functions.

How to do it...

We will build two classes to represent game-tree with the help of the following steps:

1. Create the abstract class `Move`:

    ```
    using UnityEngine;
    using System.Collections;

    public abstract class Move
    {
    }
    ```

2. Create the pseudo-abstract class `Board`:

    ```
    using UnityEngine;
    using System.Collections;

    public class Board
    {
        protected int player;
        //next steps here
    }
    ```

3. Define the default constructor:

    ```
    public Board()
    {
        player = 1;
    }
    ```

4. Implement the virtual function for retrieving the next possible moves:

```
public virtual Move[] GetMoves()
{
    return new Move[0];
}
```

5. Implement the virtual function for playing a move on the board:

```
public virtual Board MakeMove(Move m)
{
    return new Board();
}
```

6. Define the virtual function for testing whether the game is over:

```
public virtual bool IsGameOver()
{
    return true;
}
```

7. Implement the virtual function for retrieving the current player:

```
public virtual int GetCurrentPlayer()
{
    return player;
}
```

8. Implement the virtual function for testing the board's value for a given player:

```
public virtual float Evaluate(int player)
{
    return Mathf.NegativeInfinity;
}
```

9. Also, implement the virtual function for testing the board's value for the current player:

```
public virtual float Evaluate()
{
    return Mathf.NegativeInfinity;
}
```

How it works...

We have created the stepping stones for the next algorithms. The `Board` class works as a node to represent the current game state, and the `Move` class to represent an edge. When the `GetMoves` function is called, we model the function for getting the edges to reach the neighbors of the current game state.

See also

For more theoretical insights about the techniques in this chapter, please refer to Russel and Norvig's *Artificial Intelligence: A Modern Approach* (adversarial search) and Ian Millington's *Artificial Intelligence for Games* (board games).

Implementing Minimax

Minimax is an algorithm based on minimizing the possible loss for the worst case (maximum loss). Besides game development and game theory, Minimax is a decision rule that is also used in statistics, decision theory, and philosophy.

This technique was originally formulated for the two-player zero-sum game theory, meaning that one player's win is the opponent's loss. However, in this case, it is flexible enough to handle more than two players.

Getting ready...

It is important to know the difference between a dynamic member function and a static member function, as well as recursion. A dynamic member function is bound to the instance of the class, while the static member function is bound to the class itself. The static method allows us to call it without instantiating an object. This is great for general-purpose algorithms, such as the ones we'll be developing in this recipe.

In the case of recursion, it's not always clear (differing with iteration) that this is an iterative process that requires a base case (also called the stop condition) and a recursive case (the one to keep iterating).

How to do it...

We will create the base class for handling all of our main algorithms and implement the `Minimax` function as follows:

1. Create the `BoardAI` class:

   ```
   using UnityEngine;
   using System.Collections;

   public class BoardAI
   {

   }
   ```

2. Declare the `Minimax` function:

   ```
   public static float Minimax(
           Board board,
           int player,
           int maxDepth,
           int currentDepth,
           ref Move bestMove)
   {
       // next steps here
   }
   ```

3. Consider the base case:

   ```
   if (board.IsGameOver() || currentDepth == maxDepth)
       return board.Evaluate(player);
   ```

4. Set the initial values depending on the player:

   ```
   bestMove = null;
   float bestScore = Mathf.Infinity;
   if (board.GetCurrentPlayer() == player)
       bestScore = Mathf.NegativeInfinity;
   ```

5. Loop through all the possible moves and return the best score:

   ```
   foreach (Move m in board.GetMoves())
   {
       // next steps here
   }
   return bestScore;
   ```

6. Create a new game state from the current move:

```
Board b = board.MakeMove(m);
float currentScore;
Move currentMove = null;
```

7. Start the recursion:

```
currentScore = Minimax(b, player, maxDepth, currentDepth + 1, ref
currentMove);
```

8. Validate the score for the current player:

```
if (board.GetCurrentPlayer() == player)
{
    if (currentScore > bestScore)
    {
        bestScore = currentScore;
        bestMove = currentMove;
    }
}
```

9. Validate the score for the adversary:

```
else
{
    if (currentScore < bestScore)
    {
        bestScore = currentScore;
        bestMove = currentMove;
    }
}
```

How it works...

The algorithm works as a bounded **Depth-First Search** (**DFS**). In each step, the move is chosen by selecting the option that maximizes the player's score and assuming the opponent will choose the option of minimizing it until a terminal (leaf) node is reached.

The move tracking is done using recursion, and the heuristic for selecting or assuming an option depends on the `Evaluate` function.

See also

For further information, please refer to the following material:

- *Working the game-tree class* recipe in this chapter

Implementing Negamax

When we have a zero-sum game with only two players involved, we are able to improve Minimax, taking advantage of the principle that one player's loss is the other's gain. In this way, it is able to provide the same results as the Minimax algorithm. However, it does not track whose move it is. Negamax is an improvement from Minimax.

Getting ready...

It is important to know the difference between a dynamic member function and a static member function, as well as recursion. A dynamic member function is bound to the instance of the class, while a static member function is bound to the class itself. The static method allows us to call it without instantiating an object. This is great for general-purpose algorithms, such as the one we are developing in this recipe.

In the case of recursion, it's not always clear (differing with iteration) that this is an iterative process that requires a base case (also called the stop condition) and a recursive case (the one to keep iterating).

How to do it...

We will add a new function to the `BoardAI` class as follows:

1. Create the `Negamax` function:

```
public static float Negamax(
        Board board,
        int maxDepth,
        int currentDepth,
        ref Move bestMove)
{
    // next steps here
}
```

2. Validate the base case:

```
if (board.IsGameOver() || currentDepth == maxDepth)
    return board.Evaluate();
```

3. Set the initial values:

```
bestMove = null;
float bestScore = Mathf.NegativeInfinity;
```

4. Loop through all the available moves and return the best score:

```
foreach (Move m in board.GetMoves())
{
    // next steps here
}
return bestScore;
```

5. Create a new game state from the current move:

```
Board b = board.MakeMove(m);
float recursedScore;
Move currentMove = null;
```

6. Start the recursion:

```
recursedScore = Negamax(b, maxDepth, currentDepth + 1, ref
currentMove);
```

7. Set the current score and update the best score and move, if necessary:

```
float currentScore = -recursedScore;
if (currentScore > bestScore)
{
    bestScore = currentScore;
    bestMove = m;
}
```

How it works...

The base algorithm works the same, but we're making some improvements. At each step of going back in the recursion, the scores from the previous steps have their sign inverted. Instead of choosing the best option, the algorithm changes the sign of the score, eliminating the need for tracking whose move it is.

There's more...

As Negamax alternates the viewpoints between players at each step, the evaluate function used is the one with no parameters.

See also

For further exploration and understanding, please refer to the following material:

- *Working the game-tree class* recipe in this chapter
- *Implementing Minimax* recipe in this chapter

Implementing AB Negamax

There is still room for improving the Negamax algorithm. Despite its efficiency, the downside of the Negamax algorithm is that it examines more nodes than is necessary (for example, board positions). To overcome this problem, we use Negamax with a search strategy called alpha-beta pruning.

Getting ready...

It is important to know the difference between a dynamic member function and a static member function, as well as recursion. A dynamic member function is bound to the instance of the class, while the static member function is bound to the class itself. The static method allows us to call it without instantiating an object. This is great for general-purpose algorithms, such as the ones we'll be developing in this recipe.

In the case of recursion, it's not always clear (differing with iteration) that this is an iterative process that requires a base case (also called the stop condition) and a recursive case (the one to keep iterating).

How to do it...

We will add a new function to the `BoardAI` class as follows:

1. Create the `ABNegamax` function:

```
public static float ABNegamax(
```

```
                Board board,
                int player,
                int maxDepth,
                int currentDepth,
                ref Move bestMove,
                float alpha,
                float beta)
    {
         // next steps here
    }
```

2. Validate the base case:

```
if (board.IsGameOver() || currentDepth == maxDepth)
    return board.Evaluate(player);
```

3. Set the initial values:

```
bestMove = null;
float bestScore = Mathf.NegativeInfinity;
```

4. Loop through every available move and return the best score:

```
foreach (Move m in board.GetMoves())
{
    // next steps here
}
return bestScore;
```

5. Create a new game state from the current move:

```
Board b = board.MakeMove(m);
```

6. Set the values for calling the recursion:

```
float recursedScore;
Move currentMove = null;
int cd = currentDepth + 1;
float max = Mathf.Max(alpha, bestScore);
```

7. Start the recursion:

```
recursedScore = ABNegamax(b, player, maxDepth, cd, ref currentMove,
-beta, max);
```

8. Set the current score and update the best score and move if necessary. Also, stop the iteration if necessary:

```
float currentScore = -recursedScore;
if (currentScore > bestScore)
{
    bestScore = currentScore;
    bestMove = m;

    if (bestScore >= beta)
        return bestScore;
}
```

How it works...

Since we know the basic principle of the algorithm, let's concentrate on the search strategy. There are two values: alpha and beta, respectively. The alpha value is the lowest score a player can achieve, thus avoiding considering any move where the opponent has the opportunity to lessen it. Similarly, the beta value is the upper limit, and no matter how tempting the new option is, the algorithm assumes that the opponent won't provide the opportunity to take it.

Given the alternation between each player (minimizing and maximizing), only one value needs to be checked at each step.

See also

- The *Working the game-tree class* recipe
- The *Minimax* recipe
- The *Negamaxing* recipe

Implementing NegaScout

Including a search strategy also makes room for new challenges. NegaScouting is the result of narrowing the search by improving the pruning heuristic. It is based on a concept called **search window**, which is the interval between the alpha and beta values. So, reducing the search window increases the chance of a branch being pruned.

Getting ready...

It is important to know the difference between a dynamic member function and a static member function, as well as recursion. A dynamic member function is bound to the instance of the class, while the static member function is bound to the class itself. The static method allows us to call it without instantiating an object. This is great for general-purpose algorithms, such as the ones we'll be developing in this recipe.

In the case of recursion, it's not always clear (differing with iteration) that this is an iterative process that requires a base case (also called the stop condition) and a recursive case (the one to keep iterating).

How to do it...

We will add a new function to the `BoardAI` class as follows:

1. Create the `ABNegascout` function:

```
public static float ABNegascout (
        Board board,
        int player,
        int maxDepth,
        int currentDepth,
        ref Move bestMove,
        float alpha,
        float beta)
{
    // next steps here
}
```

2. Validate the base case:

```
if (board.IsGameOver() || currentDepth == maxDepth)
    return board.Evaluate(player);
```

3. Set the initial values:

```
bestMove = null;
float bestScore = Mathf.NegativeInfinity;
float adaptiveBeta = beta;
```

4. Loop through every available move and return the best score:

```
foreach (Move m in board.GetMoves())
{
    // next steps here
}
return bestScore;
```

5. Create a new game state from the current move:

```
Board b = board.MakeMove(m);
```

6. Set the values for the recursion:

```
Move currentMove = null;
float recursedScore;
int depth = currentDepth + 1;
float max = Mathf.Max(alpha, bestScore);
```

7. Call the recursion:

```
recursedScore = ABNegamax(b, player, maxDepth, depth, ref
currentMove, -adaptiveBeta, max);
```

8. Set the current score and validate it:

```
float currentScore = -recursedScore;
if (currentScore > bestScore)
{
    // next steps here
}
```

9. Validate for pruning:

```
if (adaptiveBeta == beta || currentDepth >= maxDepth - 2)
{
    bestScore = currentScore;
    bestMove = currentMove;
}
```

10. Otherwise, take a look around:

```
else
{
    float negativeBest;
    negativeBest = ABNegascout(b, player, maxDepth, depth, ref
bestMove, -beta, -currentScore);
    bestScore = -negativeBest;
}
```

11. Stop the loop if necessary. Otherwise, update the adaptive value:

```
if (bestScore >= beta)
    return bestScore;
adaptiveBeta = Mathf.Max(alpha, bestScore) + 1f;
```

How it works...

This algorithm works by examining the first move of each node. The following moves are examined using a scout pass with a narrower window based on the first move. If the pass fails, it is repeated using a full-width window. As a result, a large number of branches are pruned and failures are avoided.

See also

- The *AB Negamaxing* recipe

Implementing a Tic-Tac-Toe rival

To make use of the previous recipes, we will devise a way to implement a rival for the popular game Tic-Tac-Toe. Not only does it help us extend the base classes, but it also gives us a way to create rivals for our own board games.

Getting ready...

We will need to create a specific move class for the Tic-Tac-Toe board derived from the parent class we created at the beginning of the chapter:

```
using UnityEngine;
using System.Collections;

public class MoveTicTac : Move
{
    public int x;
    public int y;
    public int player;

    public MoveTicTac(int x, int y, int player)
    {
```

```
        this.x = x;
        this.y = y;
        this.player = player;
    }
}
```

How to do it...

We will create a new class, deriving it from `Board`, override its parent's methods, and create new ones:

1. Create the `BoardTicTac` class, deriving it from `Board`, and add the corresponding member variables for storing the board's values:

```
using UnityEngine;
using System;
using System.Collections;
using System.Collections.Generic;

public class BoardTicTac : Board
{
    protected int[,] board;
    protected const int ROWS = 3;
    protected const int COLS = 3;
}
```

2. Implement the default constructor:

```
public BoardTicTac(int player = 1)
{
    this.player = player;
    board = new int[ROWS, COLS];
    board[1,1] = 1;
}
```

3. Define the function for retrieving the next player in turn:

```
private int GetNextPlayer(int p)
{
    if (p == 1)
        return 2;
    return 1;
}
```

4. Create a function for evaluating a given position regarding a given player:

```
private float EvaluatePosition(int x, int y, int p)
{
    if (board[y, x] == 0)
        return 1f;
    else if (board[y, x] == p)
        return 2f;
    return -1f;
}
```

5. Define a function for evaluating the neighbors of a given position regarding a given player:

```
private float EvaluateNeighbours(int x, int y, int p)
{
    float eval = 0f;
    int i, j;
    for (i = y - 1; i < y + 2; y++)
    {
        if (i < 0 || i >= ROWS)
            continue;
        for (j = x - 1; j < x + 2; j++)
        {
            if (j < 0 || j >= COLS)
                continue;
            if (i == j)
                continue;
            eval += EvaluatePosition(j, i, p);
        }
    }
    return eval;
}
```

6. Implement a constructor for building new states with values:

```
public BoardTicTac(int[,] board, int player)
{
    this.board = board;
    this.player = player;
}
```

7. Override the member function for getting the available moves from the current state:

```
public override Move[] GetMoves()
{
    List<Move> moves = new List<Move>();
    int i;
    int j;
    for (i = 0; i < ROWS; i++)
    {
        for (j = 0; j < COLS; j++)
        {
            if (board[i, j] != 0)
                continue;
            MoveTicTac m = new MoveTicTac(j, i, player);
            moves.Add(m);
        }
    }
    return moves.ToArray();
}
```

8. Override the function for retrieving a new state from a given move:

```
public override Board MakeMove(Move m)
{
    MoveTicTac move = (MoveTicTac)m;
    int nextPlayer = GetNextPlayer(move.player);
    int[,] copy = new int[ROWS, COLS];
    Array.Copy(board, 0, copy, 0, board.Length);
    copy[move.y, move.x] = move.player;
    BoardTicTac b = new BoardTicTac(copy, nextPlayer);
    return b;
}
```

9. Define the function for evaluating the current state given a player:

```
public override float Evaluate(int player)
{
    float eval = 0f;
    int i, j;
    for (i = 0; i < ROWS; i++)
    {
        for (j = 0; j < COLS; j++)
        {
            eval += EvaluatePosition(j, i, player);
            eval += EvaluateNeighbours(j, i, player);
```

```
            }
        }
        return eval;
    }
```

10. Implement the function for evaluating the current state of the current player:

```
public override float Evaluate()
{
    float eval = 0f;
    int i, j;
    for (i = 0; i < ROWS; i++)
    {
        for (j = 0; j < COLS; j++)
        {
            eval += EvaluatePosition(j, i, player);
            eval += EvaluateNeighbours(j, i, player);
        }
    }
    return eval;
}
```

How it works...

We define a new type of move for the board that works well with the base algorithms because they make use of it only at a high level as a data structure. The recipe's bread and butter comes from overriding the virtual functions from the `Board` class to model the problem. We use a two-dimensional integer array for storing the players' moves on the board (0 representing an empty place), and we work out a heuristic for defining the value of a given state regarding its neighbors.

There's more...

The functions for evaluating a board's (state) score have an admissible heuristic, but it's probably not optimal. It is up to us to revisit this problem and refactor the body of the aforementioned functions to have a better-tuned rival.

See also

- The *Working the game-tree class* recipe

Implementing a Checkers rival

You will learn how to extend the previous recipes with an advanced example. In this case, you will learn how to model a Checkers (draughts) board and its pieces to comply with the necessary functions to be used with our board-AI framework.

This approach uses a chess board (of the size 8 x 8) and its respective number of pieces (12). However, it can be easily parameterized to change these values if we want to have a different-sized board.

Getting ready...

First, we need to create a new type of movement for this particular case called `MoveDraughts`:

```
using UnityEngine;
using System.Collections;

public class MoveDraughts : Move
{
    public PieceDraughts piece;
    public int x;
    public int y;
    public bool success;
    public int removeX;
    public int removeY;
}
```

This data structure stores the piece to be moved, the new x and y coordinates if the movement is a successful capture, and the position of the piece to be removed.

How to do it...

We will implement two core classes for modeling the pieces and the board, respectively. This is a long process, so it is advised to read each step carefully:

1. Create a new file called `PieceDraughts.cs` and add the following statements:

```
using UnityEngine;
using System.Collections;
using System.Collections.Generic;
```

2. Add the `PieceColor` data type:

```
public enum PieceColor
{
    WHITE,
    BLACK
};
```

3. Add the `PieceType` data enum:

```
public enum PieceType
{
    MAN,
    KING
};
```

4. Start building the `PieceDraughts` class:

```
public class PieceDraughts : MonoBehaviour
{
    public int x;
    public int y;
    public PieceColor color;
    public PieceType type;
    // next steps here
}
```

5. Define the function for setting up the piece logically:

```
public void Setup(int x, int y,
        PieceColor color,
        PieceType type = PieceType.MAN)
{
    this.x = x;
```

```
        this.y = y;
        this.color = color;
        this.type = type;
    }
```

6. Define the function for moving the piece on the board:

```
public void Move (MoveDraughts move, ref PieceDraughts [,] board)
{
    board[move.y, move.x] = this;
    board[y, x] = null;
    x = move.x;
    y = move.y;
    // next steps here
}
```

7. If the move is a capture, remove the corresponding piece:

```
if (move.success)
{
    Destroy(board[move.removeY, move.removeX]);
    board[move.removeY, move.removeX] = null;
}
```

8. Stop the process if the piece is KING:

```
if (type == PieceType.KING)
    return;
```

9. Change the type of piece if it is MAN and it reaches the opposite border:

```
int rows = board.GetLength(0);
if (color == PieceColor.WHITE && y == rows)
    type = PieceType.KING;
if (color == PieceColor.BLACK && y == 0)
    type = PieceType.KING;
```

10. Define the function for checking whether a move is inside the bounds of the board:

```
private bool IsMoveInBounds(int x, int y, ref PieceDraughts[,]
board)
{
    int rows = board.GetLength(0);
    int cols = board.GetLength(1);
```

```
        if (x < 0 || x >= cols || y < 0 || y >= rows)
            return false;
        return true;
    }
```

11. Define the general function for retrieving the possible moves:

```
public Move[] GetMoves(ref PieceDraughts[,] board)
{
    List<Move> moves = new List<Move>();
    if (type == PieceType.KING)
        moves = GetMovesKing(ref board);
    else
        moves = GetMovesMan(ref board);
    return moves.ToArray();
}
```

12. Start implementing the function for retrieving the moves when the piece's type is Man:

```
private List<Move> GetMovesMan(ref PieceDraughts[,] board)
{
    // next steps here
}
```

13. Add the variable for storing the two possible moves:

```
List<Move> moves = new List<Move>(2);
```

14. Define the variable for holding the two possible horizontal options:

```
int[] moveX = new int[] { -1, 1 };
```

15. Define the variable for holding the vertical direction depending on the piece's color:

```
int moveY = 1;
if (color == PieceColor.BLACK)
    moveY = -1;
```

16. Implement the loop for iterating through the two possible options and return the available moves. We will implement the body of the loop in the next step:

```
foreach (int mX in moveX)
{
    // next teps
}
return moves;
```

17. Declare two new variables for computing the next position to be considered:

```
int nextX = x + mX;
int nextY = y + moveY;
```

18. Test the possible option if the move is out of bounds:

```
if (!IsMoveInBounds(nextX, y, ref board))
    continue;
```

19. Continue with the next option if the move is being blocked by a piece of the same color:

```
PieceDraughts p = board[moveY, nextX];
if (p != null && p.color == color)
    continue;
```

20. Create a new move to be added to the list:

```
MoveDraughts m = new MoveDraughts();
m.piece = this;
```

21. Create a simple move if the position is available:

```
if (p == null)
{
    m.x = nextX;
    m.y = nextY;
}
```

22. Test whether the piece can be captured, and modify the move accordingly:

```
else
{
    int hopX = nextX + mX;
    int hopY = nextY + moveY;
    if (!IsMoveInBounds(hopX, hopY, ref board))
        continue;
    if (board[hopY, hopX] != null)
        continue;
    m.y = hopX;
    m.x = hopY;
    m.success = true;
    m.removeX = nextX;
    m.removeY = nextY;
}
```

23. Add the move to the list:

```
moves.Add(m);
```

24. Start to implement the function for retrieving the available moves when the piece's type is `King`:

```
private List<Move> GetMovesKing(ref PieceDraughts[,] board)
{
    // next steps here
}
```

25. Declare the variable for holding the possible moves:

```
List<Move> moves = new List<Move>();
```

26. Create the variables for searching in four directions:

```
int[] moveX = new int[] { -1, 1 };
int[] moveY = new int[] { -1, 1 };
```

27. Start implementing the loop for checking all the possible moves, and retrieve those moves. The next step will implement the body of the inner loop:

```
foreach (int mY in moveY)
{
    foreach (int mX in moveX)
    {
        // next steps here
    }
}
return moves;
```

28. Create the variables for testing the moves and advances:

```
int nowX = x + mX;
int nowY = y + mY;
```

29. Create a loop for going in that direction until the board's bounds are reached:

```
while (IsMoveInBounds(nowX, nowY, ref board))
{
    // next steps here
}
```

30. Get the position's piece reference:

```
PieceDraughts p = board[nowY, nowX];
```

31. If it is a piece of the same color, stop going further:

```
if (p != null && p.color == color)
    break;
```

32. Define a variable for creating the new available move:

```
MoveDraughts m = new MoveDraughts();
m.piece = this;
```

33. Create a simple move if the position is available:

```
if (p == null)
{
    m.x = nowX;
    m.y = nowY;
}
```

34. Test whether the piece can be captured and modify the move accordingly:

```
else
{
    int hopX = nowX + mX;
    int hopY = nowY + mY;
    if (!IsMoveInBounds(hopX, hopY, ref board))
        break;
    m.success = true;
    m.x = hopX;
    m.y = hopY;
    m.removeX = nowX;
    m.removeY = nowY;
}
```

35. Add the move and advance a step towards the current direction:

```
moves.Add(m);
nowX += mX;
nowY += mY;
```

36. Create a new class called `BoardDraughts` in a new file:

```
using UnityEngine;
using System.Collections;
using System.Collections.Generic;

public class BoardDraughts : Board
{
    public int size = 8;
```

```
        public int numPieces = 12;
        public GameObject prefab;
        protected PieceDraughts[,] board;
    }
```

37. Implement the `Awake` function:

```
void Awake()
{
    board = new PieceDraughts[size, size];
}
```

38. Start implementing the `Start` function. It is important to note that this may vary depending on your game's spatial representation:

```
void Start()
{
    // TODO
    // initialization and board set up
    // your implementation may vary

    // next steps here
}
```

39. Throw an error message if the template object doesn't have an attached `PieceDraught` script:

```
PieceDraughts pd = prefab.GetComponent<PieceDraughts>();
if (pd == null)
{
    Debug.LogError("No PieceDraught component detected");
    return;
}
```

40. Add iterator variables:

```
int i;
int j;
```

41. Implement the loop for placing the white pieces:

```
int piecesLeft = numPieces;
for (i = 0; i < size; i++)
{
    if (piecesLeft == 0)
        break;
    int init = 0;
    if (i % 2 != 0)
```

```
        init = 1;
    for (j = init; j < size; j+=2)
    {
        if (piecesLeft == 0)
            break;
        PlacePiece(j, i);
        piecesLeft--;
    }
}
```

42. Implement the loop for placing the black pieces:

```
piecesLeft = numPieces;
for (i = size - 1; i >= 0; i--)
{
    if (piecesLeft == 0)
        break;
    int init = 0;
    if (i % 2 != 0)
        init = 1;
    for (j = init; j < size; j+=2)
    {
        if (piecesLeft == 0)
            break;
        PlacePiece(j, i);
        piecesLeft--;
    }
}
```

43. Implement the function for placing a specific piece. This could change in your game depending on its visualization:

```
private void PlacePiece(int x, int y)
{
    // TODO
    // your own transformations
    // according to space placements
    Vector3 pos = new Vector3();
    pos.x = (float)x;
    pos.y = -(float)y;
    GameObject go = GameObject.Instantiate(prefab);
    go.transform.position = pos;
    PieceDraughts p = go.GetComponent<PieceDraughts>();
    p.Setup(x, y, color);
    board[y, x] = p;
}
```

44. Implement the `Evaluate` function with no parameters:

```
public override float Evaluate()
{
    PieceColor color = PieceColor.WHITE;
    if (player == 1)
        color = PieceColor.BLACK;
    return Evaluate(color);
}
```

45. Implement the `Evaluate` function with a parameter:

```
public override float Evaluate(int player)
{
    PieceColor color = PieceColor.WHITE;
    if (player == 1)
        color = PieceColor.BLACK;
    return Evaluate(color);
}
```

46. Start implementing the general function for evaluation:

```
private float Evaluate(PieceColor color)
{
    // next steps here
}
```

47. Define the variables for holding the evaluation and assigning points:

```
float eval = 1f;
float pointSimple = 1f;
float pointSuccess = 5f;
```

48. Create variables for holding the board's bounds:

```
int rows = board.GetLength(0);
int cols = board.GetLength(1);
```

49. Define variables for iteration:

```
int i;
int j;
```

50. Iterate throughout the board to look for moves and possible captures:

```
for (i = 0; i < rows; i++)
{
    for (j = 0; j < cols; j++)
    {
        PieceDraughts p = board[i, j];
        if (p == null)
            continue;
        if (p.color != color)
            continue;
        Move[] moves = p.GetMoves(ref board);
        foreach (Move mv in moves)
        {
            MoveDraughts m = (MoveDraughts)mv;
            if (m.success)
                eval += pointSuccess;
            else
                eval += pointSimple;
        }
    }
}
```

51. Retrieve the evaluation value:

```
return eval;
```

52. Start developing the function for retrieving the board's available moves:

```
public override Move[] GetMoves()
{
    // next steps here
}
```

53. Define the variables for holding the moves and the board's boundaries, and handling iteration:

```
List<Move> moves = new List<Move>();
int rows = board.GetLength(0);
int cols = board.GetLength(1);
int i;
int j;
```

54. Get the moves from all the available pieces on the board:

```
for (i = 0; i < rows; i++)
{
    for (j = 0; i < cols; j++)
    {
        PieceDraughts p = board[i, j];
        if (p == null)
            continue;
        moves.AddRange(p.GetMoves(ref board));
    }
}
```

55. Return the moves found:

```
return moves.ToArray();
```

How it works...

The board works in a similar fashion to the previous board, but it has a more complex process due to the rules of the game. The movements are tied to the piece's moves, thus creating a cascading effect that must be handled carefully. Each piece has two types of movement depending on its color and type.

As we can see, the high-level rules are the same. It just requires a little bit of patience and thinking to develop good evaluation functions and procedures for retrieving the board's available moves.

There's more...

The `Evaluate` function is far from perfect. We implemented a heuristic based solely on the number of available moves and captured the opponent's pieces, providing room for improvements to avoid movements where a player's piece could be captured on the rival's next move.

Also, we should make our own changes to the `PlacePiece` function in the `BoardDraughts` class. We implemented a direct method that probably doesn't fit your game's spatial setup.

Implementing Rock-Paper-Scissors AI with UCB1

Rock-Paper-Scissors is a classic game for testing AI techniques; that's why we'll use this case scenario for the current and following recipes. We will implement what are called **bandit algorithms** based on the notion of exploring *n*-armed bandits. It's usually modeled towards a slot machine, but we will study it as an RPS player. The main idea is to get hold of the option that results in a better payoff.

In this recipe, we will learn about the UCB1 algorithm and how it works.

Getting ready...

First, we need to implement a data structure for defining our actions:

```
public enum RPSAction
{
  Rock, Paper, Scissors
}
```

How to do it...

We will implement a `Bandit` class for building the logic behind the algorithm:

1. Create a new class named `Bandit`:

    ```
    using UnityEngine;

    public class Bandit : MonoBehaviour
    {
      // next steps
    }
    ```

2. Define the required member variables:

    ```
    bool init;
    int totalActions;
    int[] count;
    float[] score;
    int numActions;
    RPSAction lastAction;
    int lastStrategy;
    ```

3. Define the function for initializing the UCB1 algorithm:

```
public void InitUCB1()
{
  if (init)
    return;
 // next step
}
```

4. Define the local variables and initialize them:

```
totalActions = 0;
numActions = System.Enum.GetNames(typeof(RPSAction)).Length;
count = new int[numActions];
score = new float[numActions];
int i;
for (i = 0; i < numActions; i++)
{
  count[i] = 0;
  score[i] = 0f;
}
init = true;
```

5. Define a member function for computing the next action to be taken by the agent:

```
public RPSAction GetNextActionUCB1()
{
  // next steps
}
```

6. Include the required local variables:

```
int i, best;
float bestScore;
float tempScore;
InitUCB1();
```

7. Check the number of actions available. If an action hasn't been explored, return it:

```
for (i = 0; i < numActions; i++)
{
  if (count[i] == 0)
  {
    lastStrategy = i;
```

```
        lastAction = GetActionForStrategy((RPSAction)i);
        return lastAction;
    }
}
```

8. Initialize the variables for computing the best score:

```
best = 0;
bestScore = score[best]/(float)count[best];
float input = Mathf.Log(totalActions/(float)count[best]);
input *= 2f;
bestScore += Mathf.Sqrt(input);
```

9. Check all the actions available:

```
for (i = 0; i < numActions; i++)
{
    // next step
}
```

10. Compute the best score:

```
tempScore = score[i]/(float)count[i];
input = Mathf.Log(totalActions/(float)count[best]);
input *= 2f;
tempScore = Mathf.Sqrt(input);
if (tempScore > bestScore)
{
    best =i;
    bestScore = tempScore;
}
```

11. Return the best action:

```
lastStrategy = best;
lastAction = GetActionForStrategy((RPSAction)best);
return lastAction;
```

12. Define the function for retrieving the best response for a given initial action:

```
public RPSAction GetActionForStrategy(RPSAction strategy)
{
    RPSAction action;
    // next steps
}
```

13. Implement the basic rules of the game:

```
switch (strategy)
{
  default:
  case RPSAction.Paper:
    action = RPSAction.Scissors;
    break;
  case RPSAction.Rock:
    action = RPSAction.Paper;
    break;
  case RPSAction.Scissors:
    action = RPSAction.Rock;
    break;
}
```

14. Return the best action:

```
return action;
```

15. Define the member function for computing the utility of an action, based on the opponent's one. Initially, it's a draw:

```
public float GetUtility(RPSAction myAction, RPSAction opponents)
{
  float utility = 0f;
  // next steps
}
```

16. Check whether the opponent played paper:

```
if (opponents == RPSAction.Paper)
{
  if (myAction == RPSAction.Rock)
    utility = -1f;
  else if (myAction == RPSAction.Scissors)
    utility = 1f;
}
```

17. Check whether the opponent played rock:

```
else if (opponents == RPSAction.Rock)
{
  if (myAction == RPSAction.Paper)
    utility = 1f;
  else if (myAction == RPSAction.Scissors)
    utility = -1f;
}
```

18. Check whether the opponent played scissors:

```
else
{
  if (myAction == RPSAction.Rock)
    utility = -1f;
  else if (myAction == RPSAction.Paper)
    utility = 1f;
}
```

19. Return the utility value:

```
return utility;
```

How it works...

We developed our recipe using a pseudo-exploratory algorithm and stored the payoff from taking a certain action. The recipe first tests every action there is, and then keeps making moves using the formula from the UCB1 algorithm. It is good enough to be challenging, and at the same time it is defeatable because the algorithm explores different options—Thus, creating better changes for the player to improve their skills, or just to be lucky.

There's more...

We need a function for handling the overall actions of the game and informing the algorithm of the actions from the opponent. In this case, the player's actions:

```
public void TellOpponentAction(RPSAction action)
{
  totalActions++;
  float utility;
  utility = GetUtility(lastAction, action);
  score[(int)lastAction] += utility;
  count[(int)lastAction] += 1;
}
```

See also

For more theoretical reading regarding the UCB1 algorithm, please refer to the work of Prof Nathan Sturtevant, at the following URL: https://www.movingai.com/gdc14/.

Implementing regret matching

Continuing with the bandit algorithms, we will explore an improvement to the UCB1 algorithm, called regret matching. We will use the same case of playing rock-paper-scissors, but it can be repurposed for other types of games, such as fighting games.

Getting ready...

It's important to have read the previous recipe and to have taken into account the member variables and data structures. The member functions are not relevant for the purpose of this algorithm as we will implement a different set to have a different recipe, but it's based on the knowledge gained previously.

How to do it...

We will implement the following steps in the same `Bandit` class we created before.

1. Define the required member variables:

   ```
   float initialRegret = 10f;
   float[] regret;
   float[] chance;
   RPSAction lastOpponentAction;
   RPSAction[] lastActionRM;
   ```

2. Define the member function for initialization:

   ```
   public void InitRegretMatching()
   {
     if (init)
       return;
     // next steps
   }
   ```

3. Declare the local variables and initialize them:

   ```
   numActions = System.Enum.GetNames(typeof(RPSAction)).Length;
   regret = new float[numActions];
   chance = new float[numActions];
   int i;
   for (i = 0; i < numActions; i++)
   {
     regret[i] = initialRegret;
   ```

```
        chance[i] = 0f;
    }
    init = true;
```

4. Define the member function for computing the next action to be taken:

```
public RPSAction GetNextActionRM()
{
    // next steps
}
```

5. Declare the local variables and call the initialization function:

```
float sum = 0f;
float prob = 0f;
int i;
InitRegretMatching();
```

6. Explore all the available options and hold the response to be taken:

```
for (i = 0; i < numActions; i++)
{
    lastActionRM[i] = GetActionForStrategy((RPSAction)i);
}
```

7. Sum the overall regret:

```
for (i = 0; i < numActions; i++)
{
    if (regret[i] > 0f)
        sum += regret[i];
}
```

8. Return a random action if the sum is less than or equal to zero:

```
if (sum <= 0f)
{
    lastAction = (RPSAction)Random.Range(0, numActions);
    return lastAction;
}
```

9. Explore the set of actions and sum the chance of regretting them:

```
for (i = 0; i < numActions; i++)
{
 chance[i] = 0f;
  if (regret[i] > 0f)
    chance[i] = regret[i];
  if (i > 0)
    chance[i] += chance[i-1];
}
```

10. Compute a random probability and compare that to the chance of taking the actions. Return the first one to be greater than the probability computed:

```
prob = Random.value;
for (i = 0; i < numActions; i++)
{
  if (prob < chance[i])
  {
    lastStrategy = i;
    lastAction = lastActionRM[i];
    return lastAction;
  }
}
```

11. Return the last action if everything else fails:

```
return (RPSAction)(numActions-1)
```

How it works...

We explore the available options and compute the payoff of taking them. Once we have taken a certain amount of action, the algorithm adjusts and retrieves actions based on stochastic events. However, we play with chance against such actions, given the opponent's moves.

There's more...

Not only it is important to define and balance strategies, but also the results of keeping track of the opponent's actions. That's why we need to implement a member function for adding them into the mix we talked about in the previous section:

```
public void TellOpponentActionRM(RPSAction action)
{
```

```
    lastOpponentAction = action;
    int i;
    for (i = 0; i < numActions; i++)
    {
      regret[i] += GetUtility((RPSAction)lastActionRM[i], (RPSAction)action);
      regret[i] -= GetUtility((RPSAction)lastAction, (RPSAction) action);
    }
}
```

Finally, it's important to balance the strategies and the utility function. It's pretty straightforward for RPS, but it could get as complex as our game.

See also

For more theoretical reading regarding the UCB1 algorithm, please refer to the work of Prof Nathan Sturtevant at the following URL: `https://www.movingai.com/gdc14/`.

8
Learning Techniques

In this chapter, we will explore the world of machine learning through the following topics:

- Predicting actions with an N-Gram predictor
- Improving the predictor – Hierarchical N-Gram
- Learning to use a Naïve Bayes classifier
- Implementing reinforcement learning
- Implementing artificial neural networks

Introduction

In this chapter, we will explore the field of machine learning. This is a very extensive and intrinsic field in which even AAA titles have a hard time, because of the amount of time that the techniques require to be tuned and experimented with.

However, the recipes that are contained in this chapter will give us a great head start in our endeavor to learn and apply machine learning techniques to our games. They are used in several different ways, but the one feature that they are most useful for is difficulty adjustment.

Finally, it is advised that you complement these recipes by reading more theoretical books on the subject, to gain in-depth insights that lie beyond the scope of this chapter.

Predicting actions with an N-Gram predictor

Predicting actions is a great way to give players a challenge by going from random selection to selection based on past actions. One way to implement machine learning is by using probabilities to predict what the player will do next, and that's what an N-Gram predictor does.

To predict the player's next choice, N-Gram predictors hold a record of the probabilities of making particular decisions (which are usually moves), given all the combinations of the choices for the previous *n* moves.

Getting ready...

This is a recipe that makes use of general types. It is recommended that you have at least a basic understanding of how they work, because it's important that we use them well.

The first thing to do is implement a data type for holding the actions and their probabilities, which is called `KeyDataRecord`.

The `KeyDataRecord.cs` file should look like this:

```
using System.Collections;
using System.Collections.Generic;

public class KeyDataRecord<T>
{
    public Dictionary<T, int> counts;
    public int total;
    public KeyDataRecord()
    {
        counts = new Dictionary<T, int>();
    }
}
```

How to do it...

The process of building an N-Gram predictor is divided into five big steps, as follows:

1. Create the general class within a file that has the same name:

```
using System.Collections;
using System.Collections.Generic;
using System.Text;

public class NGramPredictor<T>
{
    private int nValue;
    private Dictionary<string, KeyDataRecord<T>> data;
}
```

2. Implement the constructor for initializing the member variables:

```
public NGramPredictor(int windowSize)
{
    nValue = windowSize + 1;
    data = new Dictionary<string, KeyDataRecord<T>>();
}
```

3. Implement a static function for converting a set of actions into a string key:

```
public static string ArrToStrKey(ref T[] actions)
{
    StringBuilder builder = new StringBuilder();
    foreach (T a in actions)
    {
        builder.Append(a.ToString());
    }
    return builder.ToString();
}
```

4. Define the function for registering a set of sequences:

```
public void RegisterSequence(T[] actions)
{
    string key = ArrToStrKey(ref actions);
    T val = actions[nValue - 1];
    if (!data.ContainsKey(key))
        data[key] = new KeyDataRecord<T>();
    KeyDataRecord<T> kdr = data[key];
    if (kdr.counts.ContainsKey(val))
        kdr.counts[val] = 0;
    kdr.counts[val]++;
    kdr.total++;
}
```

5. Finally, implement the function for computing the prediction of the best action to take:

```
public T GetMostLikely(T[] actions)
{
    string key = ArrToStrKey(ref actions);
    KeyDataRecord<T> kdr = data[key];
    int highestVal = 0;
    T bestAction = default(T);
    foreach (KeyValuePair<T,int> kvp in kdr.counts)
    {
        if (kvp.Value > highestVal)
        {
```

```
                    bestAction = kvp.Key;
                    highestVal = kvp.Value;
                }
            }
        return bestAction;
    }
```

How it works...

The predictor registers a set of actions according to the size of the window (the number of actions to register to make predictions) and assigns them the resulting value. For example, for a window with a size of 3, the first three are saved as a key to predict that it's possible that a fourth one may follow.

The prediction function computes how likely it is for an action to be the one that follows, given a set of previous actions. The more registered actions, the more accurate the predictor will be (with some limitations).

There's more...

It is important to consider that the object of type T must override both the ToString function and the Equals function in an admissible way for it to work correctly as an index in the internal dictionaries.

Improving the predictor – Hierarchical N-Gram

The N-Gram predictor can be improved by having a handler with several other predictors ranging from 1 to *n*, and obtaining the best possible action after comparing the best guess from each one of them.

Getting ready...

We need to make some adjustments prior to implementing the hierarchical N-Gram predictor.

Add the following member function to the NGramPredictor class:

```
public int GetActionsNum(ref T[] actions)
{
    string key = ArrToStrKey(ref actions);
    if (!data.ContainsKey(key))
        return 0;
    return data[key].total;
}
```

How to do it...

Just like the N-Gram predictor, the building of the hierarchical version is a few steps long:

1. Create the new class:

```
using System;
using System.Collections;
using System.Text;

public class HierarchicalNGramP<T>
{
    public int threshold;
    public NGramPredictor<T>[] predictors;
    private int nValue;
}
```

2. Implement the constructor for initializing member values:

```
public HierarchicalNGramP(int windowSize)
{
    nValue = windowSize + 1;
    predictors = new NGramPredictor<T>[nValue];
    int i;
    for (i = 0; i < nValue; i++)
        predictors[i] = new NGramPredictor<T>(i + 1);
}
```

3. Define a function for registering a sequence, just like its predecessor:

```
public void RegisterSequence(T[] actions)
{
    int i;
    for (i = 0; i < nValue; i++)
    {
        T[] subactions = new T[i+1];
        Array.Copy(actions, nValue - i - 1, subactions, 0, i+1);
```

```
                    predictors[i].RegisterSequence(subactions);
        }
    }
```

4. Finally, implement the function for computing the prediction:

```
public T GetMostLikely(T[] actions)
{
    int i;
    T bestAction = default(T);
    for (i = 0; i < nValue; i++)
    {
        NGramPredictor<T> p;
        p = predictors[nValue - i - 1];
        T[] subactions = new T[i + 1];
        Array.Copy(actions, nValue - i - 1, subactions, 0, i + 1);
        int numActions = p.GetActionsNum(ref actions);
        if (numActions > threshold)
            bestAction = p.GetMostLikely(actions);
    }
    return bestAction;
}
```

How it works...

The hierarchical N-Gram predictor works almost exactly like its predecessor, the difference being that it holds a set of predictors and computes each main function using its children. Each method works by decomposing the set of available actions, and, whether by registering sequences or finding out the most likely future action, each method works by decomposing the set of actions and feeding the children with them.

Learning to use Naïve Bayes classifier

Learning to use examples could be hard even for humans. For example, given a list of examples for two sets of values, it's not always easy to see the connection between them. One way of solving this problem would be to classify one set of values and then give it a try, and that's where classifier algorithms come in handy.

Naïve Bayes classifiers are prediction algorithms for assigning labels to problem instances; they apply probability and Bayes' theorem with a strong-independence assumption between the variables that are to be analyzed. One of the key advantages of Bayes' classifiers is their scalability.

Getting ready...

Since it is hard to build a general classifier, we will build ours assuming that the inputs are positive- and negative-labeled examples. So, the first thing we need to do is define the labels that our classifier will handle using an enum data structure called NBCLabel:

```
public enum NBCLabel
{
    POSITIVE,
    NEGATIVE
}
```

How to do it...

The classifier we'll build won't take long, just five steps:

1. Create the class and its member variables:

```
using UnityEngine;
using System.Collections;
using System.Collections.Generic;

public class NaiveBayesClassifier : MonoBehaviour
{
    public int numAttributes;
    public int numExamplesPositive;
    public int numExamplesNegative;

    public List<bool> attrCountPositive;
    public List<bool> attrCountNegative;
}
```

2. Define the Awake method for initialization:

```
void Awake()
{
    attrCountPositive = new List<bool>();
    attrCountNegative = new List<bool>();
}
```

3. Implement the function for updating the classifier:

```
public void UpdateClassifier(bool[] attributes, NBCLabel label)
{
    if (label == NBCLabel.POSITIVE)
    {
```

```
            numExamplesPositive++;
            attrCountPositive.AddRange(attributes);
        }
        else
        {
            numExamplesNegative++;
            attrCountNegative.AddRange(attributes);
        }
    }
```

4. Define the function for computing the Naïve probability:

```
public float NaiveProbabilities(
        ref bool[] attributes,
        bool[] counts,
        float m,
        float n)
{
    float prior = m / (m + n);
    float p = 1f;
    int i = 0;
    for (i = 0; i < numAttributes; i++)
    {
        p /= m;
        if (attributes[i] == true)
            p *= counts[i].GetHashCode();
        else
            p *= m - counts[i].GetHashCode();
    }
    return prior * p;
}
```

5. Finally, implement the function for prediction:

```
public bool Predict(bool[] attributes)
{
    float nep = numExamplesPositive;
    float nen = numExamplesNegative;
    float x = NaiveProbabilities(ref attributes,
attrCountPositive.ToArray(), nep, nen);
    float y = NaiveProbabilities(ref attributes,
attrCountNegative.ToArray(), nen, nep);
    if (x >= y)
        return true;
    return false;
}
```

How it works...

The `UpdateClassifier` function takes the example input values and stores them. This is the first function to be called. The `NaiveProbabilities` function is the one responsible for computing the probabilities for the prediction function to work. Finally, the `Predict` function is the second one to be called by us to get the results of the classification.

Implementing reinforcement learning

Imagine that we need to come up with an enemy that needs to select different actions over time as the player progresses through the game and their patterns change, or a game for training different types of pets that have free will, to some extent.

For these types of tasks, there exists a series of techniques aimed at modeling learning based on experience. One of these algorithms is *Q*-learning, which will be implemented in the following recipe.

Getting ready...

Before delving into the main algorithm, you should have certain data structures implemented. We need to define a structure for the game state, another for the game actions, and a class for defining an instance of the problem. They can coexist in the same file.

The following is an example of the data structure for defining a game state:

```
public struct GameState
{
    // TODO
    // your state definition here
}
```

The following is an example of the data structure for defining a game action:

```
public struct GameAction
{
    // TODO
    // your action definition here
}
```

Finally, we will build the data type for defining a problem instance:

1. Create the file and class:

```
public class ReinforcementProblem
{
}
```

2. Define a virtual function for retrieving a random state. Depending on the type of game we're developing, we would be interested in random states concerning the current state of the game:

```
public virtual GameState GetRandomState()
{
    // TODO
    // Define your own behaviour
    return new GameState();
}
```

3. Define a virtual function for retrieving all the available actions from a given game state:

```
public virtual GameAction[] GetAvailableActions(GameState s)
{
    // TODO
    // Define your own behaviour
    return new GameAction[0];
}
```

4. Define a virtual function for carrying out an action, and then retrieving the resulting state and reward:

```
public virtual GameState TakeAction(
        GameState s,
        GameAction a,
        ref float reward)
{
    // TODO
    // Define your own behaviour
    reward = 0f;
    return new GameState();
}
```

How to do it...

We will now implement two classes. The first one stores values in a dictionary for learning purposes and the second one actually holds the Q-learning algorithm. Go through the following steps to create the two classes:

1. Create the `QValueStore` class:

```
using UnityEngine;
using System.Collections.Generic;

public class QValueStore : MonoBehaviour
{
    private Dictionary<GameState, Dictionary<GameAction, float>>
store;
}
```

2. Implement the constructor:

```
public QValueStore()
{
    store = new Dictionary<GameState, Dictionary<GameAction,
float>>();
}
```

3. Define the function for getting the resulting value of taking an action in a game state. Carefully craft this so that an action cannot be taken in that particular state:

```
public virtual float GetQValue(GameState s, GameAction a)
{
    // TODO: your behaviour here
    return 0f;
}
```

4. Implement the function for retrieving the best action to take in a certain state:

```
public virtual GameAction GetBestAction(GameState s)
{
    // TODO: your behaviour here
    return new GameAction();
}
```

5. Implement the function for the following:

```
public void StoreQValue(
        GameState s,
        GameAction a,
        float val)
```

```
    {
        if (!store.ContainsKey(s))
        {
            Dictionary<GameAction, float> d;
            d = new Dictionary<GameAction, float>();
            store.Add(s, d);
        }
        if (!store[s].ContainsKey(a))
        {
            store[s].Add(a, 0f);
        }
        store[s][a] = val;
    }
```

6. Let's move on to create the `QLearning` class that will run the algorithm:

```
using UnityEngine;
using System.Collections;

public class QLearning : MonoBehaviour
{
    public QValueStore store;
}
```

7. Define the function for retrieving random actions from a given set:

```
private GameAction GetRandomAction(GameAction[] actions)
{
    int n = actions.Length;
    return actions[Random.Range(0, n)];
}
```

8. Implement the learning function. Be advised that this is split into several steps. Start by defining it. Take into consideration that this is a coroutine:

```
public IEnumerator Learn(
        ReinforcementProblem problem,
        int numIterations,
        float alpha,
        float gamma,
        float rho,
        float nu)
{
    // next steps
}
```

9. Validate that the store list is initialized:

```
if (store == null)
    yield break;
```

10. Get a random state:

```
GameState state = problem.GetRandomState();
for (int i = 0; i < numIterations; i++)
{
    // next steps
}
```

11. Return `null` for the current frame to keep running:

```
yield return null;
```

12. Validate against the length of the walk:

```
if (Random.value < nu)
    state = problem.GetRandomState();
```

13. Get the available actions from the current game state:

```
GameAction[] actions;
actions = problem.GetAvailableActions(state);
GameAction action;
```

14. Get an action depending on the value of the randomness of exploration:

```
if (Random.value < rho)
    action = GetRandomAction(actions);
else
    action = store.GetBestAction(state);
```

15. Calculate the new state for taking the selected action on the current state and the resulting reward value:

```
float reward = 0f;
GameState newState;
newState = problem.TakeAction(state, action, ref reward);
```

16. Get the q value, given the current game, and take action, and the best action for the new state that was computed before:

```
float q = store.GetQValue(state, action);
GameAction bestAction = store.GetBestAction(newState);
float maxQ = store.GetQValue(newState, bestAction);
```

17. Apply the *Q*-learning formula:

```
q = (1f - alpha) * q + alpha * (reward + gamma * maxQ);
```

18. Store the computed `q` value, giving its parents as indices:

```
store.StoreQValue(state, action, q);
state = newState;
```

How it works...

In the *Q*-learning algorithm, the game world is treated as a state machine. It is important to bear in mind the meaning of the parameters:

- `alpha`: This is the learning rate
- `gamma`: This is the discount rate
- `rho`: This is the randomness of exploration
- `nu`: This is the length of the walk

Implementing artificial neural networks

Imagine that we made an enemy or game system that emulates the way the brain works. That's how neural networks operate. They are based on the neuron—we call it the `Perceptron`—and are formed of the sum of several neurons; its inputs and outputs are what makes a neural network.

In this recipe, we will learn how to build a neural system, starting from the `Perceptron` through to the way that they can be joined to create a network.

Getting ready...

We will need a data type for handling raw input; this is called `InputPerceptron`:

```
public class InputPerceptron
{
    public float input;
    public float weight;
}
```

How to do it...

We will implement two big classes. The first one is the implementation for the `Perceptron` data type, and the second one is the data type handling the neural network. Go through the following steps to implement these two classes:

1. Implement a `Perceptron` class derived from the `InputPerceptron` class that was previously defined:

```
public class Perceptron : InputPerceptron
{
    public InputPerceptron[] inputList;
    public delegate float Threshold(float x);
    public Threshold threshold;
    public float state;
    public float error;
}
```

2. Implement the constructor for setting the number of inputs:

```
public Perceptron(int inputSize)
{
    inputList = new InputPerceptron[inputSize];
}
```

3. Define the function for processing the inputs:

```
public void FeedForward()
{
    float sum = 0f;
    foreach (InputPerceptron i in inputList)
    {
        sum += i.input * i.weight;
    }
    state = threshold(sum);
}
```

4. Implement the functions for adjusting weights:

```
public void AdjustWeights(float currentError)
{
    int i;
    for (i = 0; i < inputList.Length; i++)
    {
        float deltaWeight;
        deltaWeight = currentError * inputList[i].weight * state;
        inputList[i].weight = deltaWeight;
```

```
        error = currentError;
    }
}
```

5. Define a function for funneling the weights with regard to the type of input:

```
public float GetIncomingWeight()
{
    foreach (InputPerceptron i in inputList)
    {
        if (i.GetType() == typeof(Perceptron))
            return i.weight;
    }
    return 0f;
}
```

6. Create the class for handling the set of `Perceptron` elements as a network:

```
using UnityEngine;
using System.Collections;

public class MLPNetwork : MonoBehaviour
{
    public Perceptron[] inputPer;
    public Perceptron[] hiddenPer;
    public Perceptron[] outputPer;
}
```

7. Implement the function for transmitting inputs from one end of the neural network to the other:

```
public void GenerateOutput(Perceptron[] inputs)
{
    int i;
    for (i = 0; i < inputs.Length; i++)
        inputPer[i].state = inputs[i].input;
    for (i = 0; i < hiddenPer.Length; i++)
        hiddenPer[i].FeedForward();
    for (i = 0; i < outputPer.Length; i++)
        outputPer[i].FeedForward();
}
```

8. Define the function for propelling the computation that actually emulates learning:

```
public void BackProp(Perceptron[] outputs)
{
    // next steps
}
```

9. Traverse the output layer for computing values:

```
int i;
for (i = 0; i < outputPer.Length; i++)
{
    Perceptron p = outputPer[i];
    float state = p.state;
    float error = state * (1f - state);
    error *= outputs[i].state - state;
    p.AdjustWeights(error);
}
```

10. Traverse the internal `Perceptron` layers:

```
for (i = 0; i < hiddenPer.Length; i++)
{
    Perceptron p = outputPer[i];
    float state = p.state;
    float sum = 0f;
    for (i = 0; i < outputs.Length; i++)
    {
        float incomingW = outputs[i].GetIncomingWeight();
        sum += incomingW * outputs[i].error;
        float error = state * (1f - state) * sum;
        p.AdjustWeights(error);
    }
}
```

11. Implement a high-level function for ease of use:

```
public void Learn(
        Perceptron[] inputs,
        Perceptron[] outputs)
{
    GenerateOutput(inputs);
    BackProp(outputs);
}
```

How it works...

We implemented two types of `Perceptron` to define the ones that handle external input and the ones internally connected to one another. That's why the basic `Perceptron` class derives from the latter one. The `FeedForward` function handles the inputs and irrigates them along the network. Finally, the function for back propagation is the one responsible for adjusting the weights. This *weight adjustment* is the emulation of learning.

Procedural Content Generation

9

In this chapter, we will learn different techniques for procedural content generation with the following recipes:

- Creating mazes with Depth-First Search
- Implementing the constructive algorithm for dungeons and islands
- Generating landscapes
- Using N-Grams for content generation
- Generating enemies with the evolutionary algorithm

Introduction

We can define **Procedural Content Generation (PCG)** in games as the creation of content via algorithms, with or without human input. It's a topic of interest for both academia and the industry, the latter ranging from big development studios to small independent developers. It can be used for generating vegetation, delivering high-level details, creating complete mazes and worlds to explore, and increasing the title's replay value, and hours of gameplay.

The different techniques covered in this chapter will give us a glimpse of the possibilities, and guide us in the right direction for more in-depth work.

Creating mazes with Depth-First Search

We will start our journey with PCG by using a search algorithm as a starting point for creating mazes. We will use the foundations acquired in `Chapter 2`, *Navigation*, and twist them a little, to create mazes.

Getting ready

For the graph, we will use the grid representation, and Boolean values to define whether a cell is a wall or not, respectively.

How to do it...

We will comprise everything in just a class that will handle the abstract representation, called DSFDungeon:

1. Define the DFSDungeon component and its member values:

```
using UnityEngine;
using System.Collections.Generic;

public class DFSDungeon : MonoBehaviour
{
  public int width;
  public int height;
  public bool[,] dungeon;
  public bool[,] visited;
  private Stack<Vector2> stack;
  private Vector2 current;
  private int size;

  // next steps
}
```

2. Define the initialization function:

```
private void Init()
{
  // next steps
}
```

3. Initialize the required variables and random initial position:

```
stack = new Stack<Vector2>();
size = width * height;
dungeon = new bool[height, width];
visited = new bool[height, width];
current.x = Random.Range(0, width - 1);
current.y = Random.Range(0, height - 1);
```

4. Assign a wall to all the cells in the dungeon:

```
int i, j;
for (j = 0; j < height; j++)
   for (i = 0; i < width; i++)
      dungeon[j, i] = true;
```

5. Insert the initial position into the stack:

```
stack.Push(current);
i = (int)current.x;
j = (int)current.y;
```

6. Mark that cell as visited, reducing the number of available cells:

```
visited[j, i] = true;
size--;
```

7. Define the member function for getting the eight connected neighbors for a given cell:

```
private Vector2[] GetNeighbors(Vector2 node)
{
   // next steps
}
```

8. Initialize the necessary variables for defining the top-left and bottom-right corners to be traversed:

```
List<Vector2> neighbors = new List<Vector2>();
int originX, targetX, originY, targetY;
originX = (int)node.x - 1;
originY = (int)node.y - 1;
targetX = (int)node.x + 1;
targetY = (int)node.y + 1;
int i, j;
```

9. Iterate through the cells and add only the valid and available cells:

```
for (j = originY; j < targetY; j++)
{
   if (j < 0 || j >= height)
      continue;
   for (i = originX; i < targetX; i++)
   {
      if (i < 0 || i >= width)
      if (i == node.x && j == node.y)
         continue;
```

```
      if (visited[j,i])
        continue;
      neighbors.Add(new Vector2(i, j));
    }
  }
```

10. Retrieve the neighbors as an array:

```
return neighbors.ToArray();
```

11. Define the function for building the maze:

```
public void Build()
{
  Init();
  // next steps
}
```

12. Iterate while there still are available positions:

```
while (size > 0)
{
  // next steps
}
```

13. Get the neighbors for the current cell:

```
Vector2[] neighbors = GetNeighbors(current);
```

14. Validate whether the number of neighbors is greater than zero:

```
if (neighbors.Length > 0)
{
  // next step
}
```

15. If so, add the current cell to the stack:

```
stack.Push(current);
```

16. Select a random neighbor and remove the wall between that neighbor and the current cell:

```
int rand = Random.Range(0, neighbors.Length - 1);
Vector2 n = neighbors[rand];
int i, j;
i = (int)current.y;
j = (int)current.x;
dungeon[j, i] = false;
```

```
i = (int)n.y;
j = (int)n.x;
dungeon[j, i] = false;
```

17. Mark the neighbor as visited:

```
visited[j, i] = true;
current = n;
size--;
```

18. Get a new position from the stack, if the stack still has elements:

```
else if (stack.Count > 0)
  current = stack.Pop();
```

How it works...

We use the principles from DFS to traverse the graph. That is, we use a stack to store cells and add or remove them accordingly. We start by defining all the cells as walls, and then, from a random position, start taking them down. We repeat the process until we have traversed the whole graph.

Implementing the constructive algorithm for dungeons and islands

One of the most-used world structures in games, besides open worlds, are dungeons. In this recipe, we will use a technique that will allow us to create both.

Getting ready

This technique works easily with a grid graph, like the one we used with the DFS maze builder. However, we will experiment with a different approach to show you how to handle space partitioning and size storage.

How to do it...

We will need to create two different classes: one for handling the nodes, and one for handling the whole tree and high-level operations.

Let's start with the node file:

1. **Create a new class named** DungeonNode2D:

```
using UnityEngine;
using System.Collections.Generic;

[System.Serializable]
public class DungeonNode2D
{
  // next steps
}
```

2. **Define its member variables:**

```
public Rect area;
public Rect block;
public Dungeon2D root;
public DungeonNode2D left;
public DungeonNode2D right;
protected int depth;
```

3. **Implement its constructor for initialization:**

```
public DungeonNode2D (Rect area, Dungeon2D root, int depth = 0)
{
this.area = area;
this.root = root;
this.depth = depth;
this.root.leaves.Add(this);
if (!this.root.tree.ContainsKey(depth))
  this.root.tree.Add(depth, new List<DungeonNode2D>());
this.root.tree[depth].Add(this);
}
```

4. **Implement the member function for splitting the node:**

```
public void Split(Dungeon2D.Split splitCall)
{
  this.root.leaves.Remove(this);
  Rect[] areas = splitCall(area);
  if (areas == null)
    return;
  left = new DungeonNode2D(areas[0], root, depth + 1);
  right = new DungeonNode2D(areas[1], root, depth + 1);
}
```

5. Implement the member function for creating a block (walkable space or cell):

```
public void CreateBlock()
{
  block = new Rect();
  block.xMin = Random.Range(area.xMin, area.center.x);
  block.yMin = Random.Range(area.yMin, area.center.y);
  block.xMax = Random.Range(area.center.x, area.xMax);
  block.yMax = Random.Range(area.center.y, area.yMax);
}
```

Now, we will need to develop the class for building the dungeon:

1. Create a new class named Dungeon2D, deriving from MonoBehaviour:

```
using UnityEngine;
using System.Collections.Generic;

public class Dungeon2D : MonoBehaviour
{
  // next steps
}
```

2. Define the member variables required:

```
public float minAcceptSize;
public Rect area;
public Dictionary<int, List<DungeonNode2D>> tree;
public HashSet<DungeonNode2D> leaves;
public delegate Rect[] Split(Rect area);
public Split splitCall;
public DungeonNode2D root;
```

3. Implement the member function for initialization:

```
public void Init()
{
  leaves.Clear();
  tree.Clear();
  if (splitCall == null)
    splitCall = SplitNode;
  root = new DungeonNode2D(area, this);
}
```

4. Implement the member function for building the dungeon:

```
public void Build()
{
  root.Split(splitCall);
  foreach (DungeonNode2D node in leaves)
    node.CreateBlock();
}
```

5. Implement the `Awake` function for instantiating the objects for storing the leaf nodes and the branch nodes:

```
private void Awake()
{
  tree = new Dictionary<int, List<DungeonNode2D>>();
  leaves = new HashSet<DungeonNode2D>();
}
```

6. Define the default member function for splitting nodes:

```
public Rect[] SplitNode(Rect area)
{
  // next steps
}
```

7. Initialize the necessary variables:

```
Rect[] areas = null;
DungeonNode2D[] children = null;
```

8. Check whether the area's width or height are below the minimum. If so, return that area:

```
float value = Mathf.Min(area.width, area.height);
if (value < minAcceptSize)
  return areas;
```

9. Check the greater value between the width and height:

```
areas = new Rect[2];
bool isHeightMax = area.height > area.width;
float half;
```

10. Split by the height, if the height is the maximum value:

```
if (isHeightMax)
{
  half = area.height/2f;
  areas[0] = new Rect(area);
  areas[0].height = half;
  areas[1] = new Rect(area);
  areas[1].y = areas[0].y + areas[0].height;
}
```

11. Split by the width, if the width is the maximum value:

```
else
{
  half = area.width/2f;
  areas[0] = new Rect(area);
  areas[0].width = half;
  areas[1] = new Rect(area);
  areas[1].x = areas[0].x + areas[0].width;
}
```

12. Return the area for the new nodes:

```
return areas;
```

How it works...

We use a technique called **Binary-Space Partitioning (BSP)**, and the node is the bread and butter of it all, along with the split function defined.

Also, we use the main component to drive all the high-level work. However, given that the splitting happens recursively, we just need to take care of the split function for the base and recursive case, and then create the connections between the blocks.

There's more...

Given that we implemented the split function as a delegate, we can improve and fine-tune the BSP by implementing new functions and assigning them to the builder as we see fit.

For example, you could try your own split function that doesn't split by half, but with a random value using the half as the pivot.

See also

For more in-depth theories about constructive algorithms, you can check out the following material:

- *Procedural Content Generation in Games: A textbook and an overview of current research*, Noor Shaker, Julian Togelius, and Mark J Nelson (2016). Springer. ISBN 978-3-319-42714-0. (http://pcgbook.com)

Generating landscapes

Besides dungeons and mazes, landscapes are the next big thing regarding procedural content. They're the *de facto* solution for open worlds. There are several algorithms for generating landscapes, and we will learn how to implement the Square-Diamond algorithm for generating landscapes. As a matter of fact, it is a popular algorithm for creating heightmap textures.

Getting ready

In this recipe, we will keep using a grid-based graph. However, this time we won't be using it for defining walls, but for terrain height. The interesting thing about this technique is that it can be applied seamlessly for both 2D and 3D worlds.

How to do it...

We will develop our terrain generator in just a single component:

1. Create a new class named `TerrainGenerator`:

```
using UnityEngine;

public class TerrainGenerator : MonoBehaviour
{
    // next steps
}
```

2. Define the member variables required for controlling size, height, and processing:

```
[Range(3, 101)]
public int size;
[Range(0.1f, 20f)]
public float maxHeight;
protected float[,] terrain;
```

3. Implement the initialization function:

```
public void Init()
{
   if (size % 2 == 0)
     size++;
   terrain = new float[size, size];
   terrain[0, 0] = Random.value;
   terrain[0, size-1] = Random.value;
   terrain[size-1, 0] = Random.value;
   terrain[size-1, size-1] = Random.value;
}
```

4. Define the function for building the terrain. This is a huge function that implements the algorithm in the next steps of the recipe:

```
public void Build()
{
   // next steps
}
```

5. Initialize the necessary variables:

```
int step = size - 1;
float height = maxHeight;
float r = Random.Range(0, height);
```

6. Create the loop that traverses the whole grid. All the following steps for the recipe exist inside this loop:

```
for (int sideLength = size-1; sideLength >= 2; sideLength /= 2)
{
   // next steps
}
```

7. Implement the square-step loop:

```
// SQUARE
int half = size / 2;
int x, y;
for (y = 0; y < size - 1; y += sideLength)
{
  for (x = 0; x < size -1; x += sideLength)
  {
    // next step
  }
}
```

8. Compute the values for the corners:

```
float average = terrain[y,x];
average += terrain[x + sideLength, y];
average += terrain[x, y + sideLength];
average += terrain[x + sideLength, y + sideLength];
average /= 4f;
average += Random.value * 2f * height;
terrain[y + half, x + half] = average
```

9. Implement the diamond-step loop:

```
// DIAMOND
for (int j = 0; j < size - 1; j = half)
{
  for (int i = (j + half)%sideLength; i < size - 1; i +=
sideLength)
  {
    // next step
  }
}
```

10. Compute the values for the corners:

```
float average = terrain[(j-half+size)%size, i];
average += terrain[(j+half)%size,i];
average += terrain[j, (i+half)%size];
average += terrain[j,(j-half+size)%size];
average = average + (Random.value * 2f * height) - height;
terrain[j, i] = average;
```

11. Wrap values on the edge for increased smoothness. This is an optional step, but worth it if the terrain needs to be used for an infinite landscape:

```
if (i == 0)
```

```
        terrain[j, size - 1] = average;
    if (j == 0)
        terrain[size-1, i] = average;
```

12. Decrease the height value:

```
    height /= 2f;
```

How it works...

After initializing the corners with some values, we go from the outer corners, working inwards and propagating those values with some randomness.

The key thing is that by working in steps, subdividing the grid into squares and diamonds, we get a randomness similar (to some extent) to the randomness we find in landscapes in nature.

It's important to fine-tune the initial values to get better results according to our specific needs for our game.

Using N-Grams for content generation

In Chapter 8, *Learning Techniques*, we learned how N-Grams is a probabilistic language model for predicting the next item in a sequence of n-1 elements, and how it can be applied in learning techniques for predicting player behavior. However, it can also be used for procedural content generation—creating new elements by imitating the style of a given set.

In this recipe, we will use the power of N-Grams for creating new levels from a given set, thus imitating the style of the designer.

Getting ready

It's important to remind ourselves about the N-Gram predictor that we developed in Chapter 8, *Learning Techniques*, as we will use it as a tool for building levels based on the previous design—in this case, a level to be used as the main pattern.

How to do it...

We will develop three different classes: a component for our prefabs, the level predictor, and the level generator that puts everything together.

`LevelSlice` is the component to attach to the prefabs:

```
using UnityEngine;

public class LevelSlice : MonoBehaviour
{
  public string id;

  override public string ToString()
  {
    return id;
  }
}
```

Now we need to develop the predictor:

```
public class LevelPredictor : NGramPredictor<LevelSlice>
{
  public LevelPredictor(int windowSize) : base(windowSize)
  {
  }
}
```

And, finally, we develop the level generator:

```
using UnityEngine;
using System.Collections.Generic;

public class LevelGenerator : MonoBehaviour
{
  public LevelPredictor predictor;
  public List<LevelSlice> pattern;
  public List<LevelSlice> result;
  private bool isInit;

  private void Start()
  {
    isInit = false;
  }

  public void Init()
  {
    result = new List<LevelSlice>();
```

```
    predictor = new LevelPredictor(3);
    predictor.RegisterSequence(pattern.ToArray());
}

public void Build()
{
    if (isInit)
        return;
    int i;
    for (i = 0; i < pattern.Count - 1; i++)
    {
        LevelSlice slice;
        LevelSlice[] input = pattern.GetRange(0, i + 1).ToArray();
        slice = predictor.GetMostLikely(input);
        result.Add(slice);
    }
}
}
```

How it works...

We used the N-Gram predictor developed in `Chapter 8`, *Learning Techniques*, as a base for the level predictor in this recipe. This allowed us to focus on the high-level logic and let the predictor do its work.

We have an initial pattern from a level comprised of prefabs that have attached the `LevelSlice` component. Then, we use that pattern to create a new level with a similar style, and of the same size as the previous one.

It's important to put a unique identifier on each prefab for the recipe to work.

There's more...

We can use this technique to build an infinite runner with the following train of thought:

1. Store the key levels (change of world or difficulty)
2. Assign them a higher-level director to the current level builder
3. Swap initial generated levels with the new ones, or keep using pattern levels to generate more until the game finishes

As demonstrated in the research cited in the following section, this technique works well with 3-grams (as used in the recipe).

See also

For further information on how to use N-Grams for procedural content generation, and the use case applied in this recipe, please visit the following resources:

- *Implementing N-Grams for Player Prediction, Procedural Generation, and Stylized AI*, Joseph Vasquez II.
  (http://www.gameaipro.com/GameAIPro/GameAIPro_Chapter48_Implementing_N-Grams_for_Player_Prediction_Proceedural_Generation_and_Stylized_AI.pdf).
- *Linear Levels Through N-Grams*, Dahlskog, Togelius, Nelson.
  (http://julian.togelius.com/Dahlskog2014Linear.pdf).

Generating enemies with the evolutionary algorithm

So far, we have created topological algorithms, so it's time to explore a different kind of content, such as enemies.

In this recipe, we will make use of the evolutionary algorithm to create waves of enemies based on the ones that are difficult to tackle for the player.

Getting ready

We need to define the template for the enemies to focus the next section on how to implement the main evolutionary algorithm. In this case, we will use a serializable class named EvolEnemy:

```
using UnityEngine;
using UnityEngine.UI;

[System.Serializable]
public class EvolEnemy
{
  public Sprite sprite;
  public int healthInit;
  public int healthMax;
  public int healthVariance;
}
```

How to do it...

We will work on two classes: the enemy generator containing the evolutionary algorithm and the enemy controller for handling the real-time instances from the enemy templates created in the previous section. We'll also use some game logic.

We need to define the controller for such a template with `EvolEnemyController`:

1. Create the class named `EvolEnemyController`:

```
using UnityEngine;
using System;
using System.Collections;

public class EvolEnemyController :
    MonoBehaviour, IComparable<EvolEnemyController>
{
  // next steps
}
```

2. Define its member variables:

```
public static int counter = 0;
[HideInInspector]
public EvolEnemy template;
public float time;
protected Vector2 bounds;
protected SpriteRenderer _renderer;
protected BoxCollider2D _collider;
```

3. Implement the member function from the `IComparable` interface:

```
public int CompareTo(EvolEnemyController other)
{
  return other.time > time ? 0 : 1;
}
```

4. Implement the initialization function:

```
public void Init(EvolEnemy template, Vector2 bounds)
{
  this.template = template;
  this.bounds = bounds;
  Revive();
}
```

5. Implement the function for reactivating the object:

```
public void Revive()
{
  gameObject.SetActive(true);
  counter++;
  gameObject.name = "EvolEnemy" + counter;

  Vector3 newPosition = UnityEngine.Random.insideUnitCircle;
  newPosition *= bounds;
  _renderer.sprite = template.sprite;
  _collider = gameObject.AddComponent<BoxCollider2D>();
}
```

6. Implement the `Update` function:

```
private void Update()
{
  if (template == null)
    return;
  time += Time.deltaTime;
}
```

7. Implement the function for defeating the enemy with a click:

```
private void OnMouseDown()
{
 Destroy(_collider);
 gameObject.SendMessageUpwards("KillEnemy", this);
}
```

Finally, we work on the enemy generator:

1. Create a new class named `EvolEnemyGenerator`:

```
using UnityEngine;
using System.Collections.Generic;

public class EvolEnemyGenerator : MonoBehaviour
{
  // next
}
```

2. Declare all the necessary member variables:

```
public int mu;
public int lambda;
public int generations;
```

```
public GameObject prefab;
public Vector2 prefabBounds;
protected int gen;
private int total;
private int numAlive;
public EvolEnemy[] enemyList;
private List<EvolEnemyController> population;
```

3. Implement the `Start` member function:

```
private void Start()
{
  Init();
}
```

4. Declare the initialization function:

```
public void Init()
{
  // next steps
}
```

5. Declare its internal variables:

```
gen = 0;
total = mu + lambda;
population = new List<EvolEnemyController>();
int i, x;
bool isRandom = total != enemyList.Length;
```

6. Create the initial generation or wave of enemies:

```
for (i = 0; i < enemyList.Length; i++)
{
  EvolEnemyController enemy;
  enemy = Instantiate(prefab).GetComponent<EvolEnemyController>();
  enemy.transform.parent = transform;
  EvolEnemy template;
  x = i;
  if (isRandom)
    x = Random.Range(0, enemyList.Length - 1);
  template = enemyList[x];
  enemy.Init(template, prefabBounds);
  population.Add(enemy);
}
```

7. Initialize the number of enemies alive relative to the size of population:

```
numAlive = population.Count;
```

8. Define the function for creating a new generation:

```
public void CreateGeneration()
{
  // next steps
}
```

9. Check whether the number of generations created is greater than allowed:

```
if (gen > generations)
   return;
```

10. Sort the individuals in ascending order, and create a list of surviving individuals:

```
population.Sort();
List<EvolEnemy> templateList = new List<EvolEnemy>();
int i, x;
for (i = mu; i < population.Count; i++)
{
  EvolEnemy template = population[i].template;
  templateList.Add(template);
  population[i].Revive();
}
```

11. Create new individuals from the surviving types:

```
bool isRandom = templateList.Count != mu;
for (i = 0; i < mu; i++)
{
  x = i;
  if (isRandom)
    x = Random.Range(0, templateList.Count - 1);
  population[i].template = templateList[x];
  population[i].Revive();
}
```

12. Increase the number of generations, and reset the number of individuals alive:

```
gen++;
numAlive = population.Count;
```

13. Implement the function for defeating enemies:

```
public void KillEnemy(EvolEnemyController enemy)
{
  enemy.gameObject.SetActive(false);
  numAlive--;
  if (numAlive > 0)
    return;
  Invoke("CreateGeneration", 3f);
}
```

How it works...

The EvolEnemy class works as a template for defining the individual phenotype. We start by using mu and lambda for defining the size of the population, and a first wave is created at random.

Then, after each wave is defeated, the evaluation function takes place, sorting the enemies from least to best fit. The first mu number of individuals are eradicated, and offspring are created by copying the surviving population. This is called a generation.

The algorithm stops after the defined number of generations are created.

There's more...

We used EvolEnemy as a base class for defining the individuals in the population and a simple rule for sorting them. This algorithm can be improved further by defining more complex templates and phenotype definitions to take mutations into account, such as speed, color, size, and strength.

Also, the enemy controller is separated from the template, given the example created to illustrate the algorithm, and to give you more room for experimentation. However, the idea is to give you the tools to grasp the algorithm, so you can apply it in your own game, once it's well understood.

See also

For further information on the genetic algorithm and its applications in procedural content generation, you can check out the following material:

- *Artificial Intelligence: A Modern Approach* (third edition), Stuart Russel, Peter Norvig (2010), Prentice Hall.
- *Procedural Content Generation in Games: A textbook and an overview of current research*, Noor Shaker, Julian Togelius, and Mark J Nelson (2016). Springer. ISBN 978-3-319-42714-0. (`http://pcgbook.com`)

10
Miscellaneous

In this chapter, you will learn different techniques for:

- Creating and managing Scriptable Objects
- Handling random numbers better
- Building an air-hockey rival
- Implementing an architecture for racing games
- Managing race difficulty using a rubber-band system

Introduction

In this final chapter, we will be introducing new techniques and using algorithms that we have learned in the previous chapters, to create new behaviors that don't quite fit in a definite category. This is a chapter to have fun with and get another glimpse of how to mix different techniques to achieve different goals.

Creating and managing Scriptable Objects

As developers, we usually need to store and load data persistently. We've probably used some formats in the past, such as XML, JSON, and CSV via text files. As such, we know it takes development time to support changes and iterations throughout the project. Much of this data is used to set up the game and shape levels, enemies, and the whole game mechanics.

As Unity developers, we harness the power of the Inspector window via public/serialized member variables; however, it makes more sense to store these values in a persistent file—that's why the `ScriptableObject` class exists. In this recipe, we will be exploring its value.

Getting ready

We will illustrate the use of the `ScriptableObject` class by working it out as part of the recipe, *Implementing an architecture for racing games*; however, it has its own place because we believe it's important to bring to the table the reasoning behind the use of the `ScriptableObject` class.

How to do it...

1. Firstly, create a new class and call it `DriverProfile`, deriving from `ScriptableObject`, as shown in the following code:

```
using UnityEngine;
public class DriverProfile : ScriptableObject
{

}
```

2. Next, add the `CreateAssetMenu` directive on top of the class declaration, as demonstrated in the following code:

```
[CreateAssetMenu(fileName = "DProfile", menuName =
"UAIPC/DriverProfile", order = 0)]
public class DriverProfile : ScriptableObject
```

3. Finally, include the following member variables:

```
[Range(0f, 1f)]
public float skill;
[Range(0f, 1f)]
public float aggression;
[Range(0f, 1f)]
public float control;
[Range(0f, 1f)]
public float mistakes;
```

How it works...

The `ScriptableObject` abstract class helps us define what the file stores, and the `CreateAssetMenu` directive helps us create a new asset that could be included later in any of our scripts easily, as shown in the following screenshot:

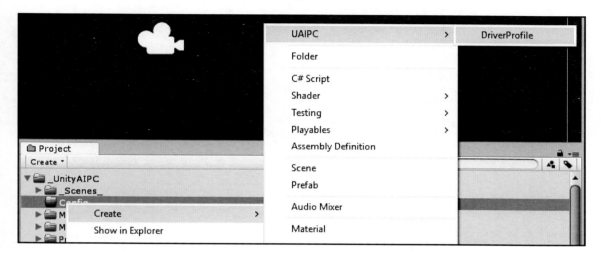

That way, we can change the configuration values as we wish, without depending on a game object, scene, or prefab, and reuse them at will; for example, having the same configuration for a couple of dummy drivers with no specific profile in our racing game, as shown in the following screenshot:

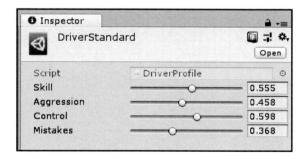

The following screenshot shows **Agent Driver** component that has a **DriverProfile** assigned:

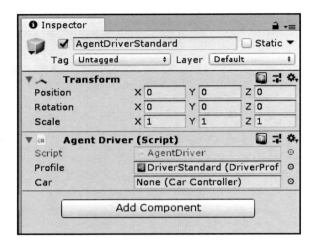

There's more...

Besides creating pluggable configurations, the `ScriptableObject` class helps us save memory space. Let's imagine we have a game object with several member variables with native types (for example, `int`, `float`, or `string`) that allocate 5 MB. To illustrate the example, let's say it's a two-dimensional array for storing a big map, among other things, and we need each enemy in the scene to have access to a copy of such a map.

If we have, let's say, 10 agents, we will be allocating 50 MB that stands for the same dataset; however, if we use a reference to an instance of a `ScriptableObject` file, we would be allocating the first 5 MB for the map, and a little more for the agents that hold a reference to the very same object.

See also

For further information on the `ScriptableObject` theory and member functions, please refer to the official documentation available online at the following addresses:

- https://docs.unity3d.com/Manual/class-ScriptableObject.html
- https://docs.unity3d.com/ScriptReference/ScriptableObject.html

Handling random numbers better

Sometimes, we need to create random behaviors that don't differ too much from a pivot point; this is the case for an **aiming behavior**. A normalized **random behavior** would shoot equally along the *x* and *y* axes, given a distance from the aiming point; however, we would like most of the bullets to aim close, because that's the expected behavior.

Most of the random functions out there return normalized values along the range given to them, and those are the expected results. Nonetheless, this is not completely useful for certain features in game development, as we just discussed. So now, we will be implementing a random function to be used in our games with normal distribution instead of a normal distribution.

Getting ready

It is important to understand the differences between uniform and normal distribution. In the following diagram, on the right-hand side, we can see a graphical representation of the behavior we're looking for by applying **normal distribution** with the example mentioned in the introductory text.

In the diagram on the left-hand side, the **uniform distribution** spreads through the whole circle, and it is aimed to be used in general random distributions; however, while developing other techniques, such as gun aiming, the desired random distribution will look more like the image on the right-hand side. Take a look at both in the following diagram:

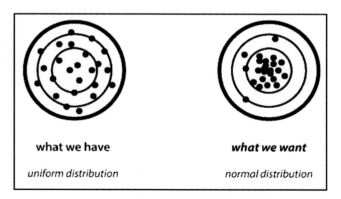

How to do it...

We will build a simple class as follows:

1. Create the `RandomGaussian` class, as shown in the following code:

```
using UnityEngine;

public class RandomGaussian
{
    // next steps
}
```

2. Define the `RangeAdditive` member function that initializes the necessary member variables, as follows:

```
public static float RangeAdditive(params Vector2[] values)
{
    float sum = 0f;
    int i;
    float min, max;
    // next steps
}
```

3. Next, check whether the number of parameters equals zero. If so, create three new values, as demonstrated in the following code:

```
if (values.Length == 0)
{
    values = new Vector2[3];
    for (i = 0; i < values.Length; i++)
        values[i] = new Vector2(0f, 1f);
}
```

4. Then, sum all the values, as shown in the following code:

```
for (i = 0; i < values.Length; i++)
{
    min = values[i].x;
    max = values[i].y;
    sum += Random.Range(min, max);
}
```

5. Finally, return the resulting random number, as follows:

```
return sum;
```

There's more...

We should always strive for efficiency. That's why there's another way to deliver a similar result. In this case, we could implement a new member function based on the solution offered by Rabin et al. (refer to the following *See also* section), as shown in the following code:

```
public static ulong seed = 61829450;
public static float Range()
{
    double sum = 0;
    for (int i = 0; i < 3; i++)
    {
        ulong holdseed = seed;
        seed ^= seed << 13;
        seed ^= seed >> 17;
        seed ^= seed << 5;
        long r = (long)(holdseed * seed);
        sum += r * (1.0 / 0x7FFFFFFFFFFFFFFF);
    }
    return (float)sum;
}
```

See also

For further information on the theory behind the Gaussian random generator and other advanced generators, please refer to the book *Game AI Pro*, by Steve Rabin, article number 3

Building an air-hockey rival

Air-hockey is probably one of the most popular games enjoyed by players of all ages during the golden age of arcades, and it is still played everywhere. With the advent of touchscreen mobile devices, developing an air-hockey game is a fun way to not only test physics engines, but to also develop intelligent rivals despite the apparent low complexity of the game.

Getting ready

This is a technique based on top of some of the algorithms that we learned in Chapter 1, *Behaviors – Intelligent Movement,* such as Seek, Arrive, and Leave, and the Raycasting knowledge that is employed in several other recipes, such as path smoothing.

It is necessary for the paddle game object to be used by the agent to have the AgentBehavior, Seek, and Leave components attached, as it is used by the current algorithm. Also, it is important to tag the objects used as walls, that is, the ones containing the box colliders, as shown in the following diagram:

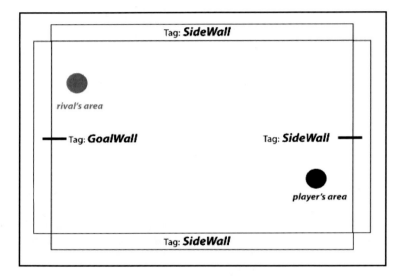

Finally, it is important to create an enum type for handling the rival's state, as shown in the following code:

```
public enum AHRState
{
    ATTACK,
    DEFEND,
    IDLE
}
```

How to do it...

This is a long class, so it is important to carefully follow these steps:

1. First, create the rival's class, as follows:

```
using UnityEngine;
using System.Collections;

public class AirHockeyRival : MonoBehaviour
{
    // next steps
}
```

2. Next, declare the public variables for setting and tuning it up, as shown in the following code:

```
public GameObject puck;
public GameObject paddle;
public string goalWallTag = "GoalWall";
public string sideWallTag = "SideWall";
[Range(1, 10)]
public int maxHits;
```

3. Declare the private variables, as follows:

```
float puckWidth;
Renderer puckMesh;
Rigidbody puckBody;
AgentBehaviour agent;
Seek seek;
Leave leave;
AHRState state;
bool hasAttacked;
```

4. Implement the `Awake` member function for setting up private classes given the public ones, as shown in the following code:

```
public void Awake()
{
    puckMesh = puck.GetComponent<Renderer>();
    puckBody = puck.GetComponent<Rigidbody>();
    agent = paddle.GetComponent<AgentBehaviour>();
    seek = paddle.GetComponent<Seek>();
    leave = paddle.GetComponent<Leave>();
    puckWidth = puckMesh.bounds.extents.z;
    state = AHRState.IDLE;
    hasAttacked = false;
```

```
            if (seek.target == null)
                seek.target = new GameObject();
            if (leave.target == null)
                leave.target = new GameObject();
        }
```

5. Declare the `Update` member function. The following code will define its body:

```
public void Update()
{
    // next steps
}
```

6. Check the current state and call the proper functions, as shown in the following code:

```
switch (state)
{
    case AHRState.ATTACK:
        Attack();
        break;
    default:
    case AHRState.IDLE:
        agent.enabled = false;
        break;
    case AHRState.DEFEND:
        Defend();
        break;
}
```

7. Call the function for resetting the active state for hitting the puck, as follows:

```
AttackReset();
```

8. Implement the function for setting up the state from external objects, as follows:

```
public void SetState(AHRState newState)
{
    state = newState;
}
```

9. Implement the function for retrieving the distance from the paddle to the puck, as shown in the following code:

```
private float DistanceToPuck()
{
    Vector3 puckPos = puck.transform.position;
```

```
        Vector3 paddlePos = paddle.transform.position;
        return Vector3.Distance(puckPos, paddlePos);
}
```

10. Declare the member function for attacking. The following code will define its body:

```
private void Attack()
{
    if (hasAttacked)
        return;
    // next steps
}
```

11. Enable the agent component and calculate the distance to the puck, as shown in the following code:

```
agent.enabled = true;
float dist = DistanceToPuck();
```

12. Check whether the puck is out of reach. If so, just follow it, as demonstrated in the following code:

```
if (dist > leave.dangerRadius)
{
    Vector3 newPos = puck.transform.position;
    newPos.z = paddle.transform.position.z;
    seek.target.transform.position = newPos;
    seek.enabled = true;
    return;
}
```

13. Attack the puck if it is within reach, as follows:

```
hasAttacked = true;
seek.enabled = false;
Vector3 paddlePos = paddle.transform.position;
Vector3 puckPos = puck.transform.position;
Vector3 runPos = paddlePos - puckPos;
runPos = runPos.normalized * 0.1f;
runPos += paddle.transform.position;
leave.target.transform.position = runPos;
leave.enabled = true;
```

14. Implement the function for resetting the parameter for hitting the puck, as shown in the following code:

```
private void AttackReset()
{
    float dist = DistanceToPuck();
    if (hasAttacked && dist < leave.dangerRadius)
        return;
    hasAttacked = false;
    leave.enabled = false;
}
```

15. Define the function for defending the goal, as follows:

```
private void Defend()
{
    agent.enabled = true;
    seek.enabled = true;
    leave.enabled = false;
    Vector3 puckPos = puckBody.position;
    Vector3 puckVel = puckBody.velocity;
    Vector3 targetPos = Predict(puckPos, puckVel, 0);
    seek.target.transform.position = targetPos;
}
```

16. Implement the function for predicting the puck's position in the future, as shown in the following code:

```
private Vector3 Predict(Vector3 position, Vector3 velocity, int
numHit)
{
    if (numHit == maxHits)
        return position;
    // next steps
}
```

17. Cast a ray given the position and the direction of the puck, as shown in the following code:

```
RaycastHit[] hits = Physics.RaycastAll(position,
velocity.normalized);
RaycastHit hit;
```

18. Check the hit results, as demonstrated in the following code:

```
foreach (RaycastHit h in hits)
{
    string tag = h.collider.tag;
    // next steps
}
```

19. Check whether it collides against the goal wall. Base case, as follows:

```
if (tag.Equals(goalWallTag))
{
    position = h.point;
    position += (h.normal * puckWidth);
    return position;
}
```

20. Check whether it collides against a side wall. Recursive case, as follows:

```
if (tag.Equals(sideWallTag))
{
    hit = h;
    position = hit.point + (hit.normal * puckWidth);
    Vector3 u = hit.normal;
    u *= Vector3.Dot(velocity, hit.normal);
    Vector3 w = velocity - u;
    velocity = w - u;
    break;
}
// end of foreach
```

21. Finally, enter the recursive case. This is done out of the `foreach` loop, as shown in the following code:

```
return Predict(position, velocity, numHit + 1);
```

How it works...

The agent calculates the puck's next hits, given its current velocity, until the calculation results in the puck hitting the agent's wall. This calculation gives a point for the agent to move its paddle toward it. Furthermore, it changes to the attack mode when the puck is close to its paddle and is moving toward it. Otherwise, it changes to become idle or to defend, depending on the new distance.

See also

For more information regarding movement and behaviors, please take a look at Chapter 1, *Behaviors – Intelligent Movement*.

Implementing an architecture for racing games

Racing games are really interesting to develop, and work on AI for the non-player drivers. They can be simple, or they can get really complex, as a car system really is tied to represent believable physics; however, there are minimum requirements for them to work, and to develop proper intelligent behaviors for non-player agents. In this recipe, we will learn how to create a small architecture for racing games.

Getting ready

We will use the driver profile object that we developed previously, and use this recipe as the cornerstone for the rubber-band system we will develop later.

How to do it...

Let's start by creating the interface to control the car. This interface is a MonoBehaviour class with public members, so the player and the agents could interact with it easily and seamlessly:

1. Create a new file and name it CarController, as shown in the following code:

   ```
   using UnityEngine;
   public class CarController : MonoBehaviour
   {
     // next steps
   }
   ```

2. Next, define the member variables, as follows:

```
public float speed;
public float maxSpeed;
public float steering;
public float maxSteering;
public Vector3 velocity;
```

3. Implement the Update for making it run and steer:

```
private void Update()
{
   transform.Rotate(Vector3.up, steering, Space.Self);
   transform.Translate(Vector3.forward * speed * Time.deltaTime,
Space.World);
}
```

Now, we will also have to work around the track nodes:

1. Create a new file and call it TrackNode, as shown in the following code:

```
using UnityEngine;

public class TrackNode : MonoBehaviour
{
   // next steps
}
```

2. Define the member variables for the node, as follows:

```
public float raceWidth;
public float offWidth;
public float wallWidth;
public TrackNode prev;
public TrackNode next;
public Vector3 normal;
```

3. Then, define the Awake function for setting it up, as shown in the following code:

```
private void Awake()
{
   // next step
}
```

4. Finally, calculate the normal vector:

```
normal = transform.forward;
if (prev != null && next != null)
{
  Vector3 nextPosition, prevPosition;
  nextPosition = next.transform.position;
  prevPosition = prev.transform.position;
  normal = nextPosition - transform.position;
  normal += transform.position - prevPosition;
  normal /= 2f;
  normal.Normalize();
}
```

How it works...

The `CarController` class is the interface we use to connect drivers and cars, just as in real life. No matter whether the driver is a real player or an AI agent, the car behaves the same, and it depends on the driver to make the most of it. We've made all the variables public, because drivers need feedback from the car; players with UI and/or the gameplay can feel, even behavior from other drivers, and AI drivers need access to that same information as well.

Managing race difficulty using a rubber-band system

We usually want to create experiences that adapt to the player, and racing games are a good field for this, given that there is the capacity for the cheater agent.

In this case, we will explore the middle ground for this by using a framework that allows you to come up with your own heuristic for managing the speed of the vehicle given its status. It doesn't matter whether it is an arcade racing game or a simulation; the framework aims to work in a similar fashion for both cases.

Getting ready

It is important to have grasped the basic skills from Chapter 1, *Behaviors – Intelligent Movement*, to be able to develop a strategy to extend the framework for your own needs, that is, understanding the principles of how the agent class works, and how the behaviors help the player move toward an object. In a nutshell, we are talking about **vector operations**.

How to do it...

We will implement three different classes for handling low-level and high-level AIs, as follows:

1. Create the class for the basic rival agent, as shown in the following code:

```
using UnityEngine;

public class RacingRival : MonoBehaviour
{
    public float distanceThreshold;
    public float maxSpeed;
    public Vector3 randomPos;
    protected Vector3 targetPosition;
    protected float currentSpeed;
    protected RacingCenter ghost;
}
```

2. Implement the Start function, as follows:

```
void Start()
{
    ghost = FindObjectOfType<RacingCenter>();
}
```

3. Define the Update function for handling the target position to follow, as shown in the following code:

```
public virtual void Update()
{
    targetPosition = transform.position + randomPos;
    AdjustSpeed(targetPosition);
}
```

4. Define your function for adjusting the speed accordingly, as you'll see in the following code:

```
public virtual void AdjustSpeed(Vector3 targetPosition)
{
    // TODO
    // your own behaviour here
}
```

5. Next, create the class for handling the ghost rider or an invincible racer, as follows:

```
using UnityEngine;

public class RacingCenter : RacingRival
{
    public GameObject player;
}
```

6. Implement the initial function for finding its target, as shown in the following code:

```
void Start()
{
    player = GameObject.FindGameObjectWithTag("Player");
}
```

7. Override the Update function, so that the invincible car can adapt to the player's behavior, as shown in the following code:

```
public override void Update()
{
    Vector3 playerPos = player.transform.position;
    float dist = Vector3.Distance(transform.position,
     playerPos);
    if (dist > distanceThreshold)
    {
        targetPosition = player.transform.position;
        base.Update();
    }
}
```

8. Implement its special behavior, as follows:

```
public override void AdjustSpeed(Vector3 targetPosition)
{

    // TODO
    // Use in case the base behaviour also applies
    base.AdjustSpeed(targetPosition);
}
```

9. Create the class for handling the high-level AI, as shown in the following code:

```
using UnityEngine;

public class Rubberband : MonoBehaviour
{
    RacingCenter ghost;
    RacingRival[] rivals;
}
```

10. Finally, assign each racer its random position in the rubber-band system. In this case, we are using a circular rubber band, as shown in the following code:

```
void Start()
{
    ghost = FindObjectOfType<RacingCenter>();
    rivals = FindObjectsOfType<RacingRival>();
    foreach (RacingRival r in rivals)
    {
        if (ReferenceEquals(r, ghost))
            continue;
        r.randomPos = Random.insideUnitSphere;
        r.randomPos.y = ghost.transform.position.y;
    }
}
```

How it works...

The high-level AI rubber band system assigns the positions to be held by the racers. Each racer has its own behavior for adjusting the speed, especially the invincible racer. This agent works as the center of the mass of the rubber band. If its speed from the player exceeds the threshold, it will adapt. Otherwise, it'll stay just the same, wobbling.

Other Books You May Enjoy

If you enjoyed this book, you may be interested in these other books by Packt:

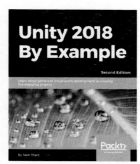

Unity 2018 By Example - Second Edition
Alan Thorn

ISBN: 9781788398701

- Understand core Unity concepts, such as game objects, components, and scenes
- Study level-design techniques for building immersive and interesting worlds
- Make functional games with C# scripting
- Use the toolset creatively to build games with different themes and styles
- Handle player controls and input functionality
- Work with terrains and world-creation tools
- Get to grips with making both 2D and 3D games

Unity 2018 Shaders and Effects Cookbook - Third Edition

John P. Doran, Alan Zucconi

ISBN: 9781788396233

- Understand physically based rendering to fit the aesthetic of your game
- Write shaders from scratch in ShaderLab and HLSL/Cg
- Combine shader programming with interactive scripts to add life to your materials
- Design efficient shaders for mobile platforms without sacrificing their realism
- Use state-of-the-art techniques, such as volumetric explosions and fur shading
- Master the math and algorithms behind the most used lighting models
- Understand how shader models have evolved and how you can create your own

Leave a review - let other readers know what you think

Please share your thoughts on this book with others by leaving a review on the site that you bought it from. If you purchased the book from Amazon, please leave us an honest review on this book's Amazon page. This is vital so that other potential readers can see and use your unbiased opinion to make purchasing decisions, we can understand what our customers think about our products, and our authors can see your feedback on the title that they have worked with Packt to create. It will only take a few minutes of your time, but is valuable to other potential customers, our authors, and Packt. Thank you!

Index